ACTIVATE

KATHERINE MILLS HERNANDEZ

D1599198

ACTIVATE

Deeper Learning Through Movement, Talk, and Flexible Classrooms

KATHERINE MILLS HERNANDEZ

FOREWORD BY JOHN MAYHER

Stenhouse
PUBLISHERS

www.stenhouse.com

PORTLAND, MAINE

Stenhouse Publishers
www.stenhouse.com

Credits
Cover design: Claramunt Group, Ltd. Co.; Interior design and typesetting: Alessandra S. Turati

Names: Hernandez, Katherine, 1972- author.
Title: Activate : deeper learning through movement, talk, and flexible
  classrooms / Katherine Hernandez.
Description: Portland, Maine : Stenhouse Publishers, 2018. | Includes
  bibliographical references. |
Identifiers: LCCN 2017049034 (print) | LCCN 2018001639 (ebook) | ISBN
  9781625311276 (ebook) | ISBN 9781625311269 (pbk. : alk. paper)
Subjects: LCSH: Active learning. | Classroom environment. | Group work in
  education. | Discussion--Study and teaching (Middle school) | Effective
  teaching. | Middle school teaching.
Classification: LCC LB1027.23 (ebook) | LCC LB1027.23 .H47 2018 (print) | DDC
  371.39--dc23
LC record available at https://lccn.loc.gov/2017049034
Manufactured in the United States of America

PRINTED ON 30% PCW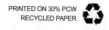
RECYCLED PAPER

24 23 22 21 20 19 18   9 8 7 6 5 4 3 2 1

Dedicated to every adult who has influenced my teaching, every child and family who has trusted me to teach and learn with them, and all my loved ones who gave me the space and encouragement to write this book.

CONTENTS

Foreword

I've often told my friends and my students that one of the things I continue to love about teaching is that it is always challenging. I can't imagine happily spending a long career at a job that I learned how to do after four or five years and where I had mostly repetition to look forward to. But even after half a century, every new teaching year brings excitement and anxiety as I wonder who these new students will be, what they will already know, and what they will want and need to learn. For me, the joy of teaching is derived from it being a constant opportunity to learn: to learn about my subject, to learn about how to teach it, to learn about my students, and perhaps most important, to learn about myself as I grow.

When I started, I didn't know that. I thought teaching was about transmitting the knowledge I'd learned in college and graduate school to students who were ready, if not always eager, to learn. It didn't take me very long to realize my mistake in the seventh-grade classes I started with; and from that moment on, I have struggled to learn with and from my students how to be the teacher they need. Right from the start, I have had some extraordinary learners in my classes who have helped me become an effective teacher. I've also learned from colleagues in the schools in which I've taught, and especially in the larger national and international network of English language arts teachers and teacher educators who continue to inform my practice and deepen my theories.

One of those learners who taught me a lot when she was a graduate student has now taught me in a new way by writing this extraordinarily insightful and deeply practical book about how to enliven and enrich and *activate* the middle school learning environment. As you will see as you read on, Katherine Mills Hernandez is an extraordinary teacher who has the ability to capture a wide range of the capacities and activities required to be the kind of teacher you want to be, and that will excite your students. She knows there is no single magic formula that will work in all schools and all classes, but by building her approach on a deep understanding of the energy dynamics of teaching and learning in classrooms, she becomes a supportive guide at your side as you build your own approaches. I sure wish I'd had her beside me as my coach during that beginning year teaching seventh grade.

Successful middle school teachers such as Katherine begin with a deep fondness for the energy of young adolescents as they make their transitions from childhood dependence to adolescent independence. And they understand that learning requires both physical and mental activity. Katherine explores how recent neuroscience research has shown the deep connections between the moving body and the active brain, and then builds a set of activities that will enable teachers and learners to exploit those connections to deepen mastery of the curriculum and enrich students' social and emotional lives. The full title and subtitle of *Activate: Deeper Learning Through Movement, Talk, and Flexible Classrooms* emphasizes the complexity and subtlety of this kind of learning-centered teaching. Some part of it was prefigured by John Dewey, but the combination of research and teaching experience that Katherine draws on provides a deeper and more practical rationale than we have ever seen before.

Engagement is the key concept in *Activate*. The engaged mind is the learning mind, and the active body deepens and enriches opportunities for engagement. Students are ultimately in charge of their own learning, but unless they are in classrooms like the ones described throughout this book, they may not recognize their controlling role. Students whose typical experiences have taken place in what I've called "commonsense" classrooms haven't had the kinds of experiences illustrated in *Activate*. They are used to teacher-centered classrooms, controlled by assignments made by teachers in response to the pressures of standardized tests developed by "experts." Such classrooms are all too rarely engaged learning spaces (Mayher 1990). And the normal effect of such commonsense teaching is transitory learning—taken in today, but forgotten soon thereafter. Engaged learning, in contrast, builds permanent changes that can then be the basis of further school learning as well as be applied to our lives out of school. I still remember projects I built and papers and stories I chose to write in middle school to this day, when most of the rest of the curriculum has vanished from my memory.

Throughout the book, Katherine makes suggestions for effective practice derived mostly from her own long experience as a middle school teacher in the public schools of New York City and schools in the Poconos of Pennsylvania. Her examples show successes, but are presented in the context of how to move slowly from a traditional teacher-centered classroom to a more learner-centered one. She does not claim to offer perfect panaceas or foolproof strategies, but illustrates how to begin and sustain the transition to an activated, engaged classroom. She demonstrates ways of getting students to move meaningfully without causing chaos. She gives guidelines for structuring meaningful talk, thereby enabling students to control their own learning by expressing their ideas and acting on the ideas of their peers. And she offers classroom design ideas that support active learning in different-sized groups and as individual learners. We hear the voices of her students and read some of their writing as they learn how to take advantage of the learning opportunities that come from movement, student-to-student talk, reading each other's writing, and being encouraged to ask questions.

To take the most advantage of this book, you might start by doing an archaeological dig into your own learning history in and out of school. What do you remember about learning in school? What sorts of things did you learn out of school? What do you remember now from either place? Who were your mentors in either context? An easy and revealing way to do this "dig" is to make a time line marked by incidents and experiences of learning and teaching, and briefly describe those that stand out (positively or negatively). If you are teaching currently, focus especially on the time in your life when you were in the same age range as your students. Some of the most engaged moments you reveal here can help you understand the power of engagement in your own learning life. Even though your students won't all learn the way you did—and do—observing their learning moments when they are or are not engaged can provide a basis for building the classroom you want.

Reading this book with deep knowledge of your own learning background will enable you to use it productively in your teaching as Katherine hopes you will.

John S. Mayher
Professor Emeritus of English Education
New York University
Adjunct Professor of English Education
Lehman College, City University of New York

Acknowledgments

C reating this book required years of learning, training, and experience in the classroom. I couldn't have written it without a grand team of people empowering me to teach in the absence of fear and with consistent attention to facilitating the best learning experiences for my students.

I have to begin, then, by acknowledging the people who gave me the foundation I needed to start off on the right foot. At New York University's Steinhardt School of Culture, Education, and Human Development, I learned from a team of caring, dedicated professors who really knew their stuff! From that team, Maureen Barbieri and John Mayher quickly became my mentors.

Maureen taught me to listen deeply, to tune in to my students, and to teach from a place of understanding them, first as humans, and secondly as learners. John taught me to back down from the pulpit I'd always perceived teachers to stand on in order to give kids the space and the tools to discuss concepts on their own.

I'm grateful to Joseph Cassidy, the principal who hired me to teach sixth-grade English Language Arts at The Clinton School for Writers and Artists, and who paired me with the Teachers College Reading and Writing Project (TCRWP) to ensure I had all the help I'd need (and more) to successfully run reading and writing workshops.

There are many people to thank at TCRWP, but at the top of the list are Mary Ehrenworth, Audra Robb, Jerry Maraia, Maggie Beattie, and Emily Strang Campbell. From running off-site workshops that inspired and informed, to getting into my classroom and coaching me toward excellence, and to bringing educators from around the country in to observe my class, these folks were my thought partners, my confidantes, my mentors, and my role models for nearly a decade. Mary taught me to teach with urgency. Audra taught me to reflect constantly. Jerry taught me to plan targeted lessons with carefully crafted teaching points. Maggie taught me to teach creatively and with grace. Emily built my confidence and helped me focus on what was working, rather than getting mired in my failures. Not all these people are still with TCRWP, but their time there deeply influenced me and the work that led to this book.

Before he was a staff developer at TCRWP, Jerry was my peer at the Clinton School and we spent many long evenings working through plans and assessments together. Emily joined us there a couple of years later and the three of us grew an unbreakable bond for which I am deeply grateful.

In my first two years at The Clinton School, I also had the honor of working with Jennifer Abrams, who was hired the same year Jerry and I came on board. The three of us were "The English Department" and leaned on each other heavily as we learned the workshop method and engaged in rigorous professional development together. Jenn had previous teaching experience and brought a lot of wisdom to the team. She also brought a great deal of passion and humor, which got us through many rough weeks with joy and laughter.

In my later years at The Clinton School, John Levin, current principal, gave me the space to teach innovatively and never questioned why my students were moving about the room so much. I'm grateful to him for trusting me. He also developed my leadership skills by expanding my role as department chair to include coaching our newest team members, Jessica Langburn and Emily Waelder (two incredible teachers and friends). John brought in the brilliant Rose Greco to coach me into this new role and I'm forever grateful to Rose for her bright mind and deep devotion to the work. John also connected me with Laura Robb, to whom I'm grateful for the wealth of knowledge and experience she's contributed to the field of literacy education, but especially for her belief in me. Laura taught me to trust my instincts, to be flexible in the classroom, to always set the kids up for success, and then to get out of their way and let them wow me!

I also want to gratefully acknowledge my coteaching partners, Dana Taylor, Heather Dasaro, and Matthew Miller, who never hesitated to follow my lead in the movement breaks, the endless room rearrangements, and the continuous work on students' discussions. And, of course, there would be no book without my nearly 1,000 students at The Clinton School. I'm grateful to each and every child who helped me learn what it means to teach him or her successfully.

When I began writing this book, I wondered if any publisher would ever deem it worthy enough to publish. Having kept in touch with Maureen Barbieri over the years, I mentioned in one of our "catching up" e-mails that I was doing some writing and she informed me that she'd recently accepted the position of acquisitions editor at Stenhouse Publishers. She encouraged me to keep writing and to send a proposal when I felt ready. The team at Stenhouse accepted my proposal, and I shouted out with joy! Over the next year and a half, Maureen worked as my editor, gently nudging my work toward clarity, accuracy, and groundedness. Later in the process, I turned to John Mayher, whom I'd also kept in contact with over the years since NYU, and whose opinion—like Maureen's—I regard deeply. He agreed to read and offer feedback on early versions of the manuscript. He talked me through the work and gave invaluable insight into rounding out the writing with increased transparency about the difficulty of achieving some of the claims I've asserted throughout. I was honored when John agreed to write the foreword.

With the writing done, the whole Stenhouse team came together to create the product you now hold in your hands. I want to thank Louisa Irele, Laurel Robinson, Grace Makley, Chandra Lowe, Zsofi

McMullin, Chuck Lerch, and Jay Kilburn for turning my manuscript into this incredible book.

Finally, none of this would have happened without the endless love and support from my family. My mother, father, and siblings encouraged me to follow my heart. I started college late and by the time I'd committed to becoming a teacher, I was married and mothering my first child. Benjamin, my husband, told me early and often, "I believe in you," and his words have bolstered me and all my decisions. Benji also works hard to ensure that all bases are covered at home, so I can focus on my work. He's the most loving and supportive partner and I could not have accomplished half of what I have without him.

Jacob, our son, took his first steps outside of John Mayher's office at NYU, on the evening of our graduation celebration from the accelerated master's program. Over the years since then, Jacob and his younger sister, Ariana, have demonstrated patience and support beyond their years, through all the weekends and evenings I've spent at my computer, working on all of my teaching preparation and assessments and on this book. They have gracefully accepted the fact that I cannot always be available for them, while honoring the time I do set aside for family togetherness, as well as our one-on-one "dates."

As a last note, I want to acknowledge the fact that you are holding this book in your hands right now. Thank you for choosing it. I hope you find great value in these pages, and that you are inspired to take even the smallest step in the direction of more deeply activating your students' engagement in their learning.

INTRODUCTION

A classroom is a magical place. It's where transformations can happen as many as fifty times each day, where epiphanies are born and inspiration sets in. The classroom is a playground for the intellect, a workshop for skill building, and a laboratory for testing new strategies. It's a place for growth, for hard work, for socialization. And it's a place where we and our students come to understand our own potential, hurdles, and motivations.

Much of our work as teachers is to plan for these miracles. We work hard to set the stage for our students to make discoveries that will ignite their own passion for learning and for doing. We choreograph intricate dances between our own goals for our students and theirs. We facilitate highly nuanced conversations that gently nudge our students toward deeper understanding of concepts and content we know they need and hope they want. We carefully navigate the currents of their curiosity, aiming to both encourage and steer it toward higher pursuits.

We diligently strive to make the content we teach match our students' interests, or at least to bridge the gap between what our students care about and what our state standards say they ought to know. We spend endless hours seeking out the perfect text and the just-right assignment, and crafting the most effective feedback, all in service of turning our kids on to learning, preserving their natural drive to grow. And our efforts do pay off. Every day we can see evidence of this: a child claims, "*Now* I get it!" and proceeds to explain in his own words his new understanding; a student hands in a paper with capital letters at the beginning and appropriate punctuation at the end of *every* sentence; our classroom is silent for a solid twenty-five minutes for the first time and we are certain that all students spent the whole time *reading* their book; a small-group lesson ends with all four students demonstrating clear progress; a student who hasn't shared her writing before suddenly raises her hand to ask, "Can I read my poem to the class?"

These are the moments that move us: they raise us up and validate all of our efforts; they remind us why we work so hard and encourage us to keep going. We hope for such moments every day, and often we see them, but if you're anything like I was a few years ago, you might be wondering how to get more of your students to experience (and demonstrate) more of these proud moments more often. Even though my students were clearly showing progress, scoring well on standardized tests, reading and writing with greater frequency, skill, and satisfaction than they had previously, and even though my administrators consistently rated my work highly, I thought my students and I could be doing more. But what was it? What could we do that I hadn't already tried? What was missing?

The answer might be surprising, but then again it might be quite obvious. As you'll learn in the first chapter of this book, I was already doing my best to apply best practices for my content area (English language arts) and was learning from the greatest teachers in our field, following the research, and working hard to improve my craft, to provide the best learning experiences I could co-create with and for my students. Still, I was aware of room for growth and was determined to discover how to sharpen the edge of our classroom experiences. I wanted to expand the reaches of the magic that was already happening for my students, and I found the answer not in a book on literacy, but in one on biology. What I discovered provided that edge, expanded the reaches of our achievement, and has forever changed my definition of the term *active engagement*.

The term is common enough in education that we've devised myriad working definitions for it. In one classroom, students are "actively engaged" when they sit and listen to a lecture. In another, they are "actively engaged" when they fill in a worksheet. In yet another classroom, "active engagement" is asking the teacher a question. I'm not convinced that we have clearly defined this term. In fact, I believe its meaning is so muddled that we can *think* our kids are actively engaged when really, they're not.

In the broadest sense, *active engagement* means *to do* something during, or just after, classroom instruction. By this definition, we might think students are actively engaged when listening to the teacher because *to listen* is *to do* something. But I propose that active engagement is achieved when students *do something that facilitates cognitive processing of course content*. "Cognitive processing of course content" can also be described as learning. By this definition, we can no longer be certain that listening to a lecture qualifies as "active engagement." How can we know if the act of listening facilitates learning? We can't. That is, we can't know until we assess the listener's understanding of the lecture. In my opinion, that leaves too much to chance. What if the student is writing notes as the teacher lectures? In this case, there is a greater chance that cognitive processing of course content (learning) is occurring. Then again, if the learner's note-taking style interferes with the stream of information coming from the teacher, then cognitive processing may be ineffective. So how can we ensure students' successful active engagement? We may need to adjust our teaching style.

We'll need to activate students' executive function (more on this later) and involve our students in tasks that align their physical actions (things they *do*—such as reading, talking, writing, using manipulatives, creating, building, and so on) with cognitive processing of course content.

Sounds like a magic trick. If not magic, then it must require a lot of effort. Right? Well, not really. It just takes some understanding of how the brain learns, a little finesse, and the willingness to try something out of the ordinary.

CONTENTS

In Chapter 1 of this book, you'll learn about my journey from wanting to do better for myself and my students to the break-throughs that transformed the way I teach, learn, and live.

Chapter 2 provides the science of how movement, talk, and a flexible environment activate executive function and prepare the brain for learning. Because the research is ongoing, I hope you'll pick up the threads and follow the leaders whose work I share in this chapter, especially those in the field of movement or exercise and its relationship with the learning brain.

You'll find strategies for increasing student movement and talk in your classroom in Chapter 3. When you see your own students more deeply engaged in your course content because you've gotten them out of their seats and given them the space for deep discussion and inquiry, I hope you'll be so impressed with the results, you'll create—along with your students—more ways to do this every day.

In Chapter 4, you'll learn a range of ways to use the physical space to stimulate students' attention and learning capacity. This can be a polarizing topic, because we know that having some element of consistency is important for young learners' sense of safety and willingness to take academic risks. However, I believe that idea has been too widely interpreted to justify never moving any furniture or reassigning areas in the classroom, creating a static space that fails to stimulate new thinking or inspire students to "go out on a limb" for learning's sake. Here, you'll see that even slight changes to your students' perception of the environment can posi-tively affect their focus when done deliberately. This section offers a lot of guidance in helping students benefit from change rather than be distracted by it. When done with care, manipulating the environment is a tool that can enhance learning, so you'll want to fold it into your repertoire.

Finally, in Chapter 5, you'll become familiar with the stages of implementation of the methods outlined in Chapters 3 and 4. You'll gain insights for navigating your way toward mastery of these practices. I aim to provide a continuum of support for you as you try these methods and gain confidence in and comfort with them. Eventually, you and your students will be able to use movement, talk, and the space intuitively to support specific classroom goals.

TEACHER AS LEARNER

One tenet of effective teaching that I embrace fervently is that the most engaging and compassionate teachers are those who practice what they preach. Doing the work we ask our students to do gives us continuous firsthand experience that serves to connect us intimately with our students' challenges and triumphs, keeps us grounded in realistic expectations for their growth and productivity, and helps deepen our bond with them. In the spirit of actively engaging in learning, then, each chapter of this book ends with suggestions for applying the concepts and strategies in your own life right away. This allows you to experience the effects I write about before ever asking your students to engage with them.

I highly recommend that you maintain a learning journal. You might keep a special notebook or digital document (though it's interesting to note that research shows that writing by hand on paper has a more profound effect on the brain and on learning than typing does), or you can devote some pages in your daily plan book just for this work. Writing reflectively is a key component in the learning process and one of the strongest ways to *actively* engage.

That brings me to another thought: you might wonder why I did not include in this book a section on writing as a tool of active engagement. The answer is simple: writing is already widely used in this way—or at least I've observed far more reflective writing in classrooms than movement or talk. The research on its effectiveness is widespread and commonly addressed in many school communities. I know math teachers who have students write to articulate their understanding of concepts; social studies teachers who have students keep learning journals, where they put into their own words what they recall from lessons and readings; science teachers who have students write to discover their questions about topics, concepts, and procedures covered in class; and literacy teachers whose students keep journals of their thoughts about reading material as well as reflections on their daily experiences. I also know principals who ask their staff members to use writing as a tool of reflection at the beginning and end of meetings.

This book, then, focuses on less ubiquitous methods that you can add to your repertoire of teaching and learning.

A final note and disclaimer of sorts: This book advocates for physical activity. I am not a doctor and make no claims about what exercises you or your students can safely do. You are responsible for your own safety and that of your students when they're in your care. My hope is that you'll encourage movement while being mindful that each person must know (or learn) his or her limits and taking care not to push anyone (including yourself) beyond that limit. Additionally, I strongly encourage partnering with your physical education colleague(s) about safety concerns and things to watch out for with your students. I'm confident that you'll see how effective small doses of movement can be for your students in the classroom. However, as you'll read in Chapter 2, the research shows that learning is most optimally enhanced after at least twenty minutes of cardiovascular exercise. So consider yourself and your students lucky if your class directly follows physical education and the kids arrive at your door with flushed cheeks, heavy breathing, and requests to visit the water fountain. All of these are signs that their brains are primed for intellectual challenge!

I've found that keeping a playful attitude smooths the transition from old habits to forming new ones. If you use the methods herein to activate your students' engagement, you and they are sure to enjoy your class more than ever before and to demonstrate a deeper connection to your course content.

And yes, you can expect improved learning outcomes and higher grades from all of your students.

CHAPTER 1

THE STORY

MY JOURNEY

I've been blessed to learn from and alongside some of the best teachers, mentors, and coaches in the field. From my highly regarded professors and mentors at New York University's Steinhardt School of Culture, Education, and Human Development to my "forever" partners at the Teachers College Reading and Writing Project, my peers and administrators at the Clinton School for Writers and Artists, and my dear coach and mentors within the New York City Department of Education, my entire career has been bolstered by incredible educators intent on helping me make every moment count for each of my students. They taught me how to examine my practice, engage and challenge the students, and make decisions with one guiding question: How does this benefit the kids as people and as learners?

All of this is to say that I was running a highly effective classroom by many standards, including (but certainly not limited to) high-stakes test scores, before embarking on the journey that led to this book. However, I knew that my students could be achieving *more* than they were and that somehow, our work wasn't all it could be. Frankly, it lacked a level of enthusiasm that I wanted my students to experience in their learning. Sure, we got excited about great literature, fun writing endeavors, and the challenges that lead to epiphanies, but I was still not convinced that my students were getting as much personal satisfaction out of their education as I thought they could. So I hit the books.

As these things happen, research in one area opened new pathways to learning in other areas. Naturally, I sought books on classroom practices first. Eventually, though, I branched off into books on adolescent brain function and the learning process and, with the grace of synchronicity, discovered a book that would change the course of my teaching, productivity, and personal management forever. That one book led to deeper research, lifestyle changes, classroom practice tweaks and overhauls, and ultimately profound improvements in engagement and learning for hundreds of students.

The book is *Spark: The Revolutionary New Science of Exercise and the Brain,* by Dr. John Ratey, an associate clinical professor of psychiatry at Harvard Medical School and internationally recognized expert in neuropsychiatry. What I learned in Ratey's book and incorporated into my own daily habits enabled me to better manage my own energy, focus, learning, and overall life experience. When I introduced these methods into the classroom, my students had similar responses. What's more, our lessons became more engaging and their work was more inspired, reflecting deeper thought and understanding.

At the heart of all these results is the undeniable connection between movement—physical exercise—and the brain's capacity to learn and retain new and complex information. We've all known for some time that exercise is good for us, but the effects it has on our brain function and specifically, on learning, were only recently discovered.

The first thing I changed in my own life was my morning routine. Instead of sleeping until the last possible moment before I *had* to drag myself out of bed each morning, I got up an hour earlier to run on my treadmill or do an intense (and fun!) dance-based aerobic workout. This set me up for an energized day, but also prepped my brain for the intellectual challenge of learning more neuroscience from an audiobook while driving ninety miles to work.

Another thing I changed was how I responded to the inevitable afternoon energy slump. Rather than shuffling to the nearest coffee vendor, I'd get some exercise. If I was blessed with a prep period, I'd run up a flight or two of stairs and briskly walk the empty school hallway (all the kids were in classrooms) to the other side of the building, then down the stairs at that end. I'd repeat as needed for three to seven minutes. If I had class with kids, the problem was addressed in our whole-class active movement breaks. If I had a meeting, I'd do some jumping jacks before leaving my classroom or do the stairs-and-hallway routine on my way to the meeting location.

I also learned to minimize the amount of time I spent in a chair (especially in the afternoons, when I was prone to tiring out). During paper-grading sessions, rather than sit at my desk, I would stand at my classroom windowsill or chest-height bookshelf or pace the room while reading my students' writing. I sat, too, but only when my body actually needed the rest.

Essentially, I'd learned to manage my energy and focus through movement. It wasn't long before I was managing my students' energy in the same ways—at least until they were able to do this on their own. More on that ahead.

Despite my challenging schedule and circumstances (that ninety-mile commute required an unusually early wake-up time), my new habits were having profound effects. I noticed little changes, at first, like not losing my train of thought in conversations, having fewer instances of "What's the word I'm looking for?," and being able to recall detailed information faster. This led to greater confidence in deep-thinking conversations with colleagues and friends. I also noticed increased clarity where I'd previously become foggy, like in those afternoon meetings aimed at solving schoolwide, grade-level, or department-specific challenges; I was better able to see the big picture and offer creative ideas for the team's consideration.

I wasn't the only one noticing these changes. My student teacher at the time (twenty years my junior) remarked on my "limitless energy" and asked if I'd discovered the fountain of youth and was willing to share my secret. My teaching partner said I'd somehow become *more* passionate about our work and that he appreciated my increased focus and creativity in planning our lessons. My husband and children said I seemed happier.

Never one to keep great news to myself, I shared my findings and personal results with everyone, including my students. I told my colleagues, friends, and family—essentially, everyone I knew—about the book and my experience of following its advice. "*Spark*" became my default answer to complaints about feeling depleted, about not making time for exercise, about getting students to break the threshold of apathy that seemed to pervade class sessions. And it was the answer to the question I was hearing more and more frequently: "How do you do it?"

To offer some perspective here, in addition to that ninety-mile commute and 3:00 a.m. wake-up, I was teaching seventh-grade English language arts as a general education teacher, writing my curriculum and creating classroom materials, chairing the department, and training as a teacher coach. Being married with two children, one in school at the time and the other a preschooler, meant that the precious hours at home were necessarily devoted to parenting and housework (except for Sundays, which I spent planning, preparing materials, and grading).

At 2:00 on a weekday afternoon, then, when my colleagues saw me teaching with energy and passion or attentively active in a sit-down meeting, or when I launched into an enthusiastic recommendation for a book I was reading, they often inquired about what kept me going and how I managed to fit it all into my crazy schedule.

The simple answer was exercise, but we all know that few things in life are as simple as a one-word answer. The longer answer? Well, that's what you're getting in this book.

Of course, this really isn't about me. My story serves only to demonstrate two things: (1) how I found my way into the powerful, effective practices that transformed my students' learning, and (2) that my confidence in these methods comes from both direct and indirect experience.

The practices have improved my own work as much as they've improved that of my students and children. I hope to hear how they work for you, too.

GETTING MY STUDENTS ON BOARD

Our class was dynamic before my students and I embarked on the practices defined in this book. As a preservice teacher, I learned to create different areas of focus in my classroom and to require students to physically move from one space to another, depending on the tasks and activities of each class session. Middle school students appreciate having chances to move about the room. The mobility affords them a greater variety of interactions and experiences in their learning activities. Because it has served our collective needs so well, a movement-rich classroom has been a mainstay of my teaching and professional development.

Having been trained in the workshop method of teaching, I'd become adept at managing student transitions from one area of the room to another. For example, kids move from our whole-class lesson "meeting area" to their independent work spaces (see Figure 1.1), and to stations reserved for group work (sometimes a small table off to the side, sometimes a space on the floor, sometimes an alcove in our classroom library). It's also common to find students sprawled around the room during reading time. In my classroom, students are not confined to one seat indefinitely.

My mentors, teachers, coaches, school administrators, and I also extol the virtues of democratic classrooms in which all students contribute meaningfully to our work. Therefore, my students are practiced at talking with one another as well as addressing the whole group, voicing their opinions, questions, discoveries, and thought processes in class every day. I've been blessed to work in a school where the noise and mess of learning and productivity are honored, yet I understand that not everyone is as privileged.

FIGURE 1.1

Class meets in the meeting area for lessons and uses the tables for independent and collaborative work.

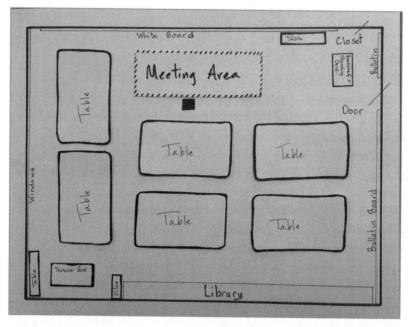

In some schools, teachers are expected to run tightly managed, quiet classrooms.

If it isn't already common knowledge, I should point out that neurologists have proved that movement and talk contribute to increased executive function (mental skills that facilitate learning)—more on this in Chapter 2—so my students were already operating at an advantage over students required to sit still and silent in a chair for forty-five minutes at a stretch. Yet, even with all of this in place, I sensed we were operating slightly below the collective potential and wanted to break through whatever barrier kept us from attaining higher ground.

As my own exercise-stimulated brain sparked new and creative ideas, I started to look at my students differently. What I'd previously observed as "engagement" started to look more like "going through the motions, but slightly disconnected from the work." To be fair, my students were engaged. They were learning, producing, and performing satisfactorily. Still, I sensed untapped energy just waiting to be activated.

One of the blessings of working with middle school kids is that it's fairly easy to "read" them, thanks to their tendency to keep their feelings and attitudes on the surface rather than mask them masterfully as older teens might do. As I watched my students shuffle into the classroom one day, I observed closely as they dropped their heavy backpacks from their shoulders—letting them bang onto tabletops, chairs, and the floor—then slumped over to unpack those backpacks, it hit me: *They're exhausted! They're lethargic! They've spent most of their day sitting in chairs! Their bodies and brains want to sleep!* I knew what I had to do to help them wake up and dive into the work of our class with renewed energy and focus.

As soon as all the students were in the room, I closed the door and called them to attention: "Stop!" I yelled, my voice demanding their attention. "Look at me." I said it sternly, so they wouldn't mistake my seriousness and carry on unpacking their bags. It worked. They immediately stopped unpacking and looked at me, anticipation freezing their faces in awkward expressions. Anyone could see they were wondering what they'd done wrong. In a cheerful-but-serious tone, I said, "Forget about the 'Do Now' and come meet me in the meeting area. I *have* to share something with you!"

To demonstrate my excitement, and to relieve them of worry that they'd violated some unknown rule, I skipped over to the meeting area with a smile on my face. Hopping in place like an impatient child, I beckoned for them to hurry.

The students looked at each other, their expressions changing from the awkward "Are we in trouble?" to the more relaxed, "Okay, she's really weird, but whatever." They shuffled over to the meeting area, sat down, and waited for my big strange news. One student called out, "What, are you gonna tell us we don't have to take any more tests for the rest of the school year?"

This caught my attention, because I rarely gave tests. "Why? Did you have a test in another class today?"

Three voices volunteered now, "We had *two* tests!" The first speaker continued, "One in math and one in science." A few of the kids groaned, and some let their heads droop under the intellectual weight of it all. "And we have a social studies project due tomorrow," another child volunteered.

I clapped my hands together and smiled even bigger. "That's *per*fect!"

Now they really looked at me like I was crazy.

"What I have to share with you right now is going to make you feel great, and it's going to help with all of your schoolwork—including tests and projects—but it isn't exactly about the schoolwork. It's about your brains."

I gave the kids a very quick overview of what I'd learned about exercise enhancing brain functions such as attention, focus, and problem solving. Then I said, "Let's try it. I want you all to get up and do some jumping jacks and stretches with me."

Now most of them were groaning (a perfect example of that middle school charm of keeping everything on the surface). Their bodies felt tired. They had been awake for too many hours. They hadn't been awake long enough yet. They hadn't gotten enough sleep the night before. They had gotten too much sleep the night before. They had run in gym the day before. They hadn't run in gym yet this week. They had eaten lunch. They hadn't eaten lunch. And on and on. I ignored all the protests and instructed them to follow along with me.

I love how kids in the middle grades respond to strange requests from teachers: unlike elementary students, who jump right in, and equally unlike older teens who seem to follow the motto "First be skeptical and resist," the middle graders pause for a moment and then participate. They're a bit quicker than high schoolers to join in once a couple of peers participate, and I've never had any students flat out refuse to try something new.

We did ten jumping jacks, then jogged in place, then danced in place, and then they followed the leader (me) around the room to walk it off. Finally we reconvened in the meeting area for stretches and deep breaths. All of this took about three and a half minutes.

"I would ask you how you feel now," I said to them, "but your laughter filled the room as we moved, you have smiles on your faces right now, and that warm color in your cheeks says that you've improved your blood flow, which means your brains are getting more oxygen, so I guess I already have my answer. Now go get your materials for today's lesson and meet me back here in five . . . four . . . three . . ." They scattered off to get their notebooks and pens and returned to the meeting area with renewed energy, focus, and purpose. I don't think it would be a stretch to say they also seemed to be full of something else that I didn't mind: appreciation for the fun break from routine.

From that moment on, my English language arts class was transformed.

The kids and I dug deeper into the course content, because it was exciting. They enjoyed learning and reaped the rewards of increased knowledge, skill, confidence, and wonder. Their grades improved. Their interests expanded. Their initiative kicked in, and their motivation was boosted. Their energized conversations spilled over into the hallways. They discovered their own reasons for pursuing more information outside of class. It was clear for all in the school community to see: the kids were ignited and inspired.

Together, my students and I built on the success of adding more deliberate movement into our class time with upgrades to our discussion protocols and using the physical space in more creative ways. As the years went on, I learned a lot about making all these components work for all kinds of kids and teaching partners. Along the way, I found the delicate balance between encouraging and overwhelming, inspiring and turning off, engaging and shutting down. My students have been incredibly willing to take this journey with me and to forgive my mishaps, accept my apologies, and let me try again when things went wrong. They helped me figure this whole thing out with patience, grace, enthusiasm, and perseverance. True to their developmental stage, they also were never afraid to tell me when something wasn't working for them. We problem-solved together and found solutions that worked for each individual and the collective. My happiest moments were when the students took ownership of their own energy and focus management, when they shared with me and their peers their breakthroughs with applying what they'd learned in our class to outside of school endeavors, and when they suggested variations for us all to try in the classroom.

I am thrilled to share with you all that my students and I learned together. Let's start with the foundation of it all: the science.

CHAPTER 2

THE SCIENCE

HOW MOVEMENT SUPPORTS LEARNING

The work of Dr. Ratey and others demonstrates that aerobic exercise causes a host of actions and reactions in the brain that lead to the birth of new neurons. Interestingly, this neurologic response to exercise is not unique to any particular age group; so far, it appears to be true for people of all ages. Given that many of us were raised with the notion that our brain cells were finite in number and susceptible to weakening over time, this news is refreshing. But what's even more relevant to educators is that those newly hatched cells are particularly prevalent in the hippocampus, which is "really important for long term memory," according to Dr. Wendy Suzuki (2011), neuroscientist and core faculty member at New York University. Further, Dr. James Phelps, psychiatrist and author of the internationally respected website PsychEducation.org, says the hippocampus "appears to be absolutely necessary for making new memories."

If exercise makes the brain grow, particularly in the area that affects learning and memory, then teachers and students have new reason to get their bodies moving throughout the school day.

The main link between exercise and the growth of new cells in the hippocampus is something called brain-derived neurotrophic factor, or BDNF. When stimulated by exercise, BDNF causes new cells to spawn, and then it works to maintain and lengthen the lives

I think moving definitely helps me learn better and it gets me motivated to learn. Seeing as I have ADHD, whenever [Mrs. H.] let us move in class it helped me a lot with my fidgeting and my extra amount of energy.
NIKKI TRACY, FORMER GRADE 6–8 STUDENT

The ways [Mrs. Hernandez] incorporated movement into our classes is especially important to me. I want to teach outdoor education because I think it is super important for kids to be frequently moving around . . . It is really important to be in touch with your body in order to be in touch with your mind.
STELLA ROSE SCHNEEBURG, FORMER GRADE 6–8 STUDENT

I always loved the walking and running around the classroom. I think part of the reason a lot of kids don't like school is because it's not very active—we're just sitting at a desk every period. Ironically, it can be pretty exhausting sitting around all day, yet the dynamic warm-ups brought something fun and new to the classroom and it helped us focus on our discussions. It didn't just feel like we were physically getting energized, but our minds were, too. I never consciously made the decision to do this, but actually, when I'm studying for a big exam, I often start walking around my house and talk to myself about that certain subject.
MANON ACHARD, FORMER GRADE 6–8 STUDENT

of those cells if they bind to meaningful information. If the new cells don't find a purpose, they will not survive. This is where things get really interesting for educators.

Exciting as this ability to grow new brain cells is, scientists tell us that simply growing new cells will not lead to an increase in intelligence, knowledge, skill, or creativity. It helps to think of exercise, then, as a first step in the process of boosting learning experiences and outcomes. Once the effects of exercise have set in and those new cells are formed and ready to bind to meaning, the brain is essentially ready to receive, process, and store new information. In other words, it's ready to learn.

For this reason, Dr. Ratey and his associates refer to exercise as "priming" the brain for learning. In *Spark: The Revolutionary New Science of Exercise and the Brain*, Ratey profiles the Naperville School District of Naperville, Illinois, which created a Learning Readiness Physical Education class (LRPE) for students in need of academic intervention. The students arrive at school an hour earlier than the general population, exercise to reach and maintain a prescribed heart rate for approximately thirty minutes, and then go directly to their remedial course. In LRPE, the kids build new brain cells and then give those cells a purpose for surviving and thriving by learning new information or skills in their instructional courses. The results are profound. All students in the program significantly improved in their area of concentration as well as in overall academic performance. (You can see the data on this district's success at the website named for their program: www.learningreadinesspe.com.)

The process of cells "binding" to something meaningful is what happens when we learn. In the face of new or complex information, those new cells respond by attaching to the new concept. That connection is reinforced every time the concept is recalled, repeated, or called into action through practice, contemplation, writing, or conversation. We can all recognize that as the repeated practice we offer students in class or the pop quizzes we assign before a big test to keep the recently learned information fresh in students' minds. Those assignments we offer actually do more than keep information fresh; they allow it to move from the temporary "working memory" to the more coveted long-term memory.

Although the story about BDNF is compelling enough, it isn't the whole story about why physical movement belongs in our classrooms. Dr. John Medina, developmental molecular biologist and author of *Brain Rules: 12 Principles for Surviving and Thriving at Work, Home, and School*, explains another reason why exercise is essential to achieving our goal of optimizing each student's learning. Exercise increases the brain's access to its main sources of energy, which are glucose and oxygen. Medina explains it this way:

> *When you exercise you increase blood flow*
> *across the tissues of your body. This is*
> *because exercise stimulates the blood vessels,*
> *which penetrate deeper into the tissues of the*
> *body. . . . The same happens in the human*
> *brain. Imaging studies have shown that*
> *exercise literally increases blood volume in a*

region of the brain called the dentate gyrus . . .
a vital constituent of the hippocampus. This
blood-flow increase, which may be the result
of new capillaries, allows more brain cells
greater access to the blood's food and haz-mat
teams. (Medina 2011, 21–22)

Great, you might be thinking, *but I don't teach PE, I teach [insert course title here], so what does this have to do with me?* To which I answer this: Schools keep kids for approximately six and a half hours, five days each week. We are responsible for their well-being as much as for their learning. Currently, PE and unstructured (or loosely structured) recess are limited to occasional, rather than daily, activities in too many schools. What's more, those occasional opportunities for students to move are frequently cut in favor of increasing seat time (usually for test prep or academic intervention). On top of that, we tend to keep students seated and quiet during the majority of class time. One way to look at this, then, is that we are contributing enormously to what Dr. James Levine (2014) of the Mayo Clinic has coined "sitting disease," which leads to a host of physical and mental problems. Another way to look at this is that by keeping our students seated and silent, we are not allowing their brains to engage at optimum levels. In effect, if we don't start getting our kids to move their bodies during class time, we're inhibiting, rather than promoting, their ability to learn.

If our students are not getting daily doses of aerobic activity, then not only is their physical well-being at risk, but their capacity to learn all the academic content we are attempt-

> *I've always had difficulty sitting in one place for a long period of time, so the runs and walks around the classroom were a way to "refresh" my brain. After we moved for a few minutes, I would be more focused on the task at hand and I would put in more effort since I was not falling asleep from being seated for so long.*
> TEODORA IVANOVIC, FORMER GRADE 6–8 STUDENT

ing to teach them is diminished. Dr. Medina writes, "Cutting off physical exercise—the very activity most likely to promote cognitive performance—to do better on a test score is like trying to gain weight by starving yourself" (Medina 2011, 25).

So long as our schools cannot guarantee a minimum of thirty minutes of exercise for each student every day, the next best thing we can do is build exercise into the classroom experience, so every child is getting powerful, effective brain (and overall health) boosts throughout the day. As a result, their moods will improve, their energy will increase, and they'll achieve greater success in their courses.

If this idea has you on edge or consumed with worry about student injuries, lawsuits, and the like, fear not. You don't need to be certified in physical education to use movement safely and effectively in the classroom. That said, I do recommend that you consult with your school's PE teacher(s), as I did, for tips and considerations about kids moving in your class. It also helps to use the same terminology the PE teachers use, so the students will make a strong connection to all they've learned in PE about safety and self-monitoring. I invited my school's PE teacher extraordinaire, Chris Jacobi, to join my class

I remember being horribly frustrated by the quality of my high school application essay, and was simply stewing at my table. That was when my teacher Mrs. Hernandez approached me with two words pouring out of her mouth, "What's wrong?"

I sighed. "My essay just isn't good, and I don't know how to fix it."

Mrs. Hernandez smiled and replied, "You should take a walk."

I stared at her dumbfounded. "A walk where?"

"Just around the classroom." Mrs. Hernandez shrugged. I continued to look blankly at her as she gestured for me to get up and go. I did. The first few steps were done with spite. . . . The next came out of uncertainty, and finally commitment. I felt my brain start processing what I could not sitting down. I completed the first lap and then went for a second. I sat back down in my chair three laps later and began to write. I looked up from my seat and saw Mrs. Hernandez smiling at me.

Now I sit as the co-chair of the New York State High School Democrats, and am on the national coordinating committee of the Young Democratic Socialists of America as their youngest committee member. I work for a political consulting firm and have my own clients, and college interns. Yet I always find time to walk. Because when I sit back down, that's when my mind starts to work and that's when I can change the world.
HANNAH ZIMMERMAN, FORMER GRADE 6–8 STUDENT

periodically and weigh in on what we were doing. This was an incredible gift that I'm sure your colleague(s) will be happy to offer as well.

Although the research shows that twenty to thirty minutes of cardiovascular movement is necessary for new cell growth, that does not preclude us from using smaller doses of exercise in the classroom to effectively boost our students' ability to focus on and process new or complex information. Dr. Medina points to one study in support of this idea in his *Brain Rules* book and Web content. It's also backed by Dr. James Levine's work. The author of *Get Up! Why Your Chair Is Killing You and What You Can Do About It* is a professor of medicine at the Mayo Clinic and principal investigator for the National Institutes of Health, which has funded Levine's three-decades–long research into the effects of sedentariness. The data indicate that we can boost cognitive activity simply by increasing oxygen supply to the brain. To do that, we just need to get ourselves and our students out of chairs and moving about.

Those of us who aren't ready to assign jumping jacks before our lectures can get kids moving in other ways to boost their learning. These won't produce the same neuron-spawning results as aerobic

In complete honesty, I was partly annoyed when we had to actually stand up and start moving around. The ecstatic tone of Mrs. Hernandez's voice and her excited jumpy movements were too much for me during an early morning class. I wanted nothing more than to collapse back in a chair and read a book to escape the cruel reality of school.

But here's the thing: just reading a book is completely different than learning from a book. You won't absorb anything from a book or lesson while being sleepy and lazy. And as the jumping around the classroom became a daily routine, I learned to appreciate the goal of Mrs. Hernandez. Similar to how you stretch your physical body before an exercise, this jumpy and wild movement warms up your brain before a lesson. Instead of sinking into my chair and being a half-conscious student, I would now sit down with my heart rapidly beating, and my mind awake and alert.

Although it took some getting used to, it became an invaluable part of the class whenever I needed to be "slapped awake." It may not seem like much, but it has a profound effect on learning for any type of class.
DAVID BLASEN, FORMER GRADE 6–8 STUDENT

exercise, but they will increase students' ability to focus and engage with our course content. The late Dr. Antronette (Toni) Yancey pointed out in her 2012 TEDx Talk, "What's Good for the Waistline Is Good for the Bottom Line," that even short bursts of activity can increase concentration, engagement, mood, self-efficacy, energy levels, cognitive processing, and morale. That is good news for any of us!

As educators, we're interested not only in improving students' ability to learn the content we have to teach them, but in boosting their ability to think for themselves, to create, integrate, collaborate, and discover the world on their own terms. We hope for them to cultivate interests into passions, to gain the ability and desire to pursue a line of thinking through research and creativity, and to examine social and world issues with discernment, intelligence, and heart. All of this requires us to provide the kind of environment in which they can develop the skills, practices, and confidence to accomplish these things. We can't do that if the kids are sitting silently in their chairs with their brains falling asleep.

Science shows us this, but I suspect each of us also knows it intuitively. How many of us do our best thinking or have our greatest epiphanies when we're standing in the shower, walking the dog, on the third mile of a run, or in the tenth breath of meditation after a challenging series of asanas? We know intuitively that when our own bodies are in motion or have just come out of challenging motion, our minds light up with clarity and creativity. Our children and students deserve the same opportunities.

In her aim to understand how exercise affects learners, Dr. Suzuki (2011) decided to turn her own graduate neurology class into an experiment. To begin, she became a certified aerobics instructor (no, I don't recommend we all do this—but go right ahead if you're inclined to), then turned her master's-level neuroscience class into a cardio-lecture course. Suzuki leads her students through an hour-long aerobic workout, then lectures for ninety minutes. The many cognitive tests her students have taken reveal a marked increase in their ability to encode new long-term memories, and her observations indicate improved attention and engagement. So far, that

ACTIVE ENGAGEMENT

Before moving on to the next section, do your favorite cardiovascular exercise for ten to twenty minutes. You can walk briskly (outdoors or on a treadmill), dance to your favorite music, hop on a pogo stick, repeatedly climb and descend a staircase, use your home gym equipment, bounce on a trampoline, alternate jumping jacks and jogging in place—you get the idea. Move your body to get your blood flowing and break a sweat.

Then, write a plan for how you'll incorporate some movement into your classes starting tomorrow (or the next time you'll be with your students).

Finally, take two to three minutes to reflect in your journal about how the movement affects you. (See Figure 2.1.) Include everything you feel physically, emotionally, and intellectually. How might this affect your students? How might it improve their learning experiences in class?

FIGURE 2.1

By journaling, I solidify my reflections and create a reference point from which to mark my growth.

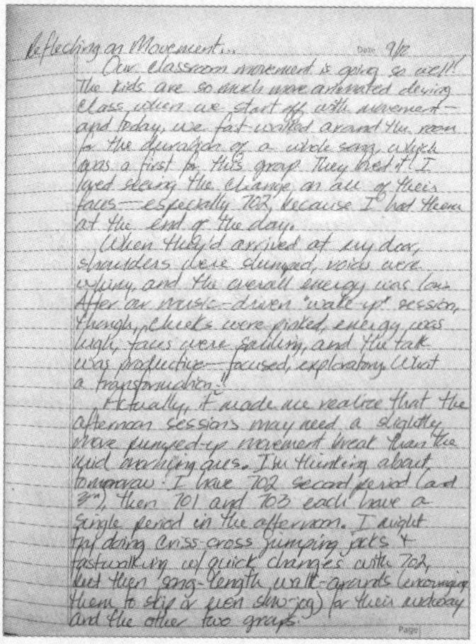

fits neatly with what we've learned from the other researchers, but Suzuki noticed an additional benefit to the exercise: a boost in creativity.

Although she said in her 2011 TEDx Talk that more research needs to be done in this area, she also said that the activity that exercise promotes in the hippocampus appears to enhance participants' ability to put "new concepts together in unique ways."

Obviously we are not going to spend an hour exercising with our students, but when we consider all of the evidence before us, it is easy to see that any time we devote to this is going to benefit our students, ourselves, and the entire school community.

In Chapter 3, you'll find suggestions for using movement in class. They range from minimal to more robust and include tips for introducing the concepts and activities to your students as well as tips about management and safety.

HOW TALK ENHANCES LEARNING

Just as science shows us the effects of movement on the brain, empirical classroom studies show the effects of talk on memory.

Every time our students have to retrieve from memory something they've learned, they reinforce that learning. This is common knowledge at this point and is the basis for all the repetition we incorporate into our lessons and assessments. What gets less attention in the academic arena is how valuable talk is to constructing knowledge in the first place.

When we encounter new information and talk about it, the processes involved in articulating our preliminary understanding serve to build meaning around the new content and convert it into tangible signals that can be stored in memory and later recalled. This can also happen with writing about the new material, but inviting conversation is far more expedient and comprehensive, because it invites various perspectives, contexts, and opportunities to question and explore.

When we allow our students multiple opportunities to speak and listen to one another in the process of learning new information, we effectively engage more of their brainpower in the task of understanding the content and then committing it to memory (see Figure 2.2). In his book *Opening Minds: Using Language to Change Lives*, Peter Johnston writes, "Through conversations," students gain an "awareness that making sense often requires more than one person" (Johnston 2012, 59).

FIGURE 2.2
When students can discuss classroom content, they integrate those concepts into working memory and co-construct meaning and relevance.

As my colleagues at the Teachers College Reading and Writing Project have proved beyond the shadow of a doubt, even small doses of talk among students have powerful effects on their learning. They showed me how to incorporate "turn-and-talk" activities into my whole-class lessons. These are brief bursts of deliberate, focused talk between two or three student partners that allow them to say, in their own words, what they know, want to know, or think they understand about what was just taught. Powerful and effective as these are, more than just the processing functions of the brain are at play when we ask our students to talk in this way; there is also a palpable effect on their attention to the material.

In the course of a fifteen-minute lesson, for example, students who sit and silently ingest the material have a more difficult time attending to the concepts the teacher is attempting to convey than do students who stop listening at intervals to speak, write, or otherwise engage with the content of the lesson by using their own language faculties. This could be in part because of the mind's tendency to wander when it's not actively engaged. What's more, when passive students go home and attempt to engage independently with the material they think they've learned, they often struggle. They discover a void in their understanding where actively engaged students (the ones who talked or wrote deliberately about the content during the lesson) have a working memory of the material and can more easily attend to the homework task.

Interestingly, the person who is best positioned to deepen his or her learning during a traditional classroom lesson is the teacher. It's the teacher, after all, who is dynamically engaged in the course content throughout the lesson—retrieving information from memory, articulating ideas through speech; writing; sketching images, charts, and diagrams; and (usually) moving around the room—while students sit still to watch and listen. When we disrupt this model of teaching and learning to get our students doing more of what the traditional teacher has done, we set them up for greater success.

Teachers who know this ask their students to engage frequently throughout a class session. These teachers might talk uninterrupted for five minutes or so and then say, "Take a moment to think about all I've just shared with you, then turn to your partner and say what you understand. This is a good time to share your questions, too." The teacher who is practiced at this method will listen in to one or two partnerships and gauge carefully when the students have had just enough time to articulate their ideas—anywhere from thirty seconds to two minutes, depending on a range of variables— and then will call the students back to attention. At that point, the teacher may invite one or two questions, but will be careful to keep moving forward in a focused manner to finish the lesson and move on to more extended student engagement. Alternatively, a teacher might pause the lesson to ask students to write, in their own words, what they understand so far and what they are wondering. This, too, would be a brief interjection.

Although these short bouts of verbal interaction are powerful, we need to also allow for longer conversations. According to Dr. Neil Mercer (2010), emeritus professor of education (specializing in the role of language in the classroom) at the University of Cambridge, in England, learners need time to pose their questions, explore the content in depth, and, in his words, practice "speaking the subject."

This idea goes back more than two millennia and is still as relevant a tool as it was when Socrates employed it. Students learn content deeply when they are allowed the time to develop questions about it, explore possible uses for it, create and solve problems with it, and hear out differing opinions about it. If we're always concerned with moving on to the next topic before students have fully digested the first and incorporated it into their own thinking repertoire, then we do them a disservice and simultaneously convey to them that we don't value true learning as highly as we do the abstract and arbitrary notion of "covering content" (specifically, content that will be tested—still too often tested for recall rather than for understanding).

Ironically, when we hold back on deep student engagement (for fear of not "covering" all the content that's considered imperative to pass the course or standardized test), we essentially rob students of the very experiences that would help them not only learn the material, but also build the skills that support overall success. Allowing for brief and extended discussions, and time to ask and respond to questions of perspective and context (Johnston 2012), and hosting these conversations in a variety of group sizes from partnerships to whole class, provides opportunities

Talking with my peers helped a lot because it would provide new ideas and new ways to approach certain problems, tasks, etc. In English, a variety of literature is read, and I think it's important for students to analyze on their own. However, it's also beneficial to be exposed to different interpretations because it will broaden their understanding of that piece of writing.
TEODORA IVANOVIC,
FORMER GRADE 6–8 STUDENT

for our students to build communication skills such as conversing with people from a variety of backgrounds, supporting ideas with evidence, considering multiple perspectives, revising their thinking in light of new ideas presented by others, and extending their understanding of the topic at hand. Talk, then, is a crucial component of the learning process, not only because it contributes to more robust learning, but also because it shapes the way our students think about course content (Vygotsky and Kozulin 1986).

We do well to provide discussion time for our students when content is fresh, such as before and after a lecture, mini-lesson, or reading, because this talk contributes to the formation of thoughts around the topic. "One of the most powerful ways to teach children to think," writes Lucy Calkins, "is to teach them to engage in thoughtful discussions that incorporate thinking under, between, and around texts" (Calkins 2014, 23). Teaching them to thoughtfully discuss concepts encountered in class means demonstrating for students how talk partners listen and respond to one another, how they present and defend arguments and interpretations, how they back up their statements with evidence, how they question and explore, and how they dig deeper. These things are not innate, but learned. Dr. Catherine O'Connor refers to them as "talk moves" (Wordgen.serpmedia.org) with which students can gain competence and confidence in practice. Of course, providing the space in our classrooms for students to converse with one another does more than shape their thinking about the subject matter. It also builds community, understanding, and empathy (Barbieri 1995).

When students listen to one another and share their ideas—whether new or developed—they gain deeper understanding, not just of the course content, but of each other. They learn how to relate and can surprise one another as they converse. By watching and listening to peers, each student gains an edge over first impressions, which can be wrong, and the chance to appreciate the complexities within each of us.

Another opportunity that comes to light during peer-centered discussions is the chance to use domain-specific vocabulary meaningfully and in an authentic context.

Time and research have proved that the ages-old method of writing lists of words and their definitions, putting them into sentences that may or may not have any bearing on the richer context of the subject, and then memorizing those words and definitions does not constitute any meaningful learning (Baker, Simmons, and Kameenui 1995). More often than not, the words and their definitions were forgotten by the following week. We've realized that words have to be used authentically, in conversations and in writing, if they're to become a part of a person's thinking and learning. We've also learned that learning fewer words well has longer-lasting results than "covering" many words superficially. Vocabulary instruction has evolved to include a variety of ways for students to engage with and study new words (Robb 1999; Marzano 2009) while folding the words into the classroom discourse: the teacher uses the words frequently in lessons and talks, keeps the words visibly posted in the room and refers to them often, and encourages and then requires students to use the words in classroom talk and all written work related to the subject they inform (Allen 1999). In conversations, when students are required to employ the words, when they hear them used accurately and then insert them into their own speeches, they adopt the meaning of words and phrases that then become a part of their broader working memory and inform the thoughts they formulate about the entirety of the subject in the context of their own lives. It is through conversations, then, that our students can begin to think in the terms of the subject. This is demonstrated in the student conversation transcribed later in this chapter.

Talking with my peers about ideas we were learning in class helped me have new insight on the topics we were learning and see how others perceived ideas. I think teenagers are extremely smart in the ways that they think, and hearing from other kids my age sometimes even helped me understand things better.
NIKKI TRACY, FORMER GRADE 6–8 STUDENT

Building on this concept, Dr. Robin Alexander of the University of Cambridge developed the practice of dialogic teaching. He shares how the interactions between teacher and student in extended conversations contribute to collective learning. Alexander's research reveals that when a teacher and student hold a discussion in front of the whole class, there are measurable benefits for all the students in the class. Instinctively, many of us might balk at the notion of one student "dominating" the talk space in a class session, but Alexander helps us see that, when done right, this is a highly effective method. In fact, Alexander points out, it's far superior to the all-too-common practice of low-level questioning, which occurs when a teacher asks a close-ended question and students compete (by raising their hands and hoping to be called upon) for the chance to showcase their knowledge of the "right" answer. This method "requires children to report someone else's thinking rather than to think for themselves, and to be judged on their accuracy or compliance in doing so" (Tharp and Gallimore 1988).

In the dialogic talk model that Dr. Alexander recommends, the student engaging in a long conversation with the teacher gets in-depth practice "speaking the subject" with the expert (the teacher). The teacher uses open-ended questions to nudge the student's thinking along and encourages deeper exploration of the topic. He or she then responds to the student's statements with an open mind and an appreciation for the thinking process the student demonstrates. The students observing the conversation hear the expert and apprentice using language effectively as a tool to push their thinking, which serves as a model for how to engage in similar work.

Making room for long one-on-one dialogue in the class will pay off, but our students also need for us to provide frequent opportunities for each of them to speak. One of my favorite ways to ensure that all students have a chance to "try on" the language of our course is to create small discussion groups that I can coach as needed. As students discuss the course content, I listen in

Work(ing) collaboratively has been something that helps me a lot. . . . By talking to my peers, I am able to both expand my thinking and see new perspectives on ideas that, while I may or may not agree with them, I can begin to understand how different backgrounds in life can lead to different interpretations.
CALLEY CRAIG, FORMER GRADE 6–8 STUDENT

and occasionally interject to offer the language that will help them communicate their meaning more clearly. These discussions can last anywhere from ten to twenty minutes, depending on available time and the goal or purpose for the talk.

The following is a snippet from one such discussion. To help you visualize the scene, my thirty-two eighth-grade students were standing around the room in groups of five or six, discussing a variety of issues from a novel we'd read as a whole class. We'd pushed most of the tables to the outermost rim of the room, leaving only a few out in the open for students to stand around during discussions. The space was opened up for more freedom of movement. A couple of groups stood in circles rather than at a table. All group members were on their feet facing one another, which allowed them to engage their bodies, activate their brains, and make eye contact. This particular activity took place during a unit of study in which one of our foci was to develop the skills of holding respectful and productive discussions about difficult (and often polarizing) subjects. I'm sharing a moment in one group's discussion when I stepped in to lure the students back to the talk strategies we'd studied and practiced earlier in the unit.

STUDENT DISCUSSION ABOUT *HATE LIST* BY JENNIFER BROWN

In this novel, the main character, Valerie, and her boyfriend, Nick, create a list of people and things they hate. Though Valerie thought the list was an end in itself—a place to vent their frustrations—Nick has a very different idea. He brings a gun to school and opens fire in the cafeteria, targeting people on the list. Here, my students discuss the shooting event and the actions of a teacher, Mr. Kline, who attempted to protect his students, but was shot and killed in the effort.

> RAY: *He didn't have to do that, though. I mean, that teacher could've reached for the gun.*

CARLA: *How can you even say that? You don't know how much space was between him and Nick.*

DEANNA: *Yeah, and anyway, I really don't think he had a lot of time to think about what to do. He just . . . acted, you know what I mean?*

RAY: *Oh, come on, he was right there in front of Nick, and instead of reaching for the gun, he just held his arms in front of the other students, as if that was going to help them. If you can't see that, then you must be blind.*

KEENAN: *Or stupid.*

ME: *Let's pause for a second. [Students look at me.] It sounds like you've found yourselves at a point of disagreement.*

RAY: *Yeah, they can't see what's so obvious!*

ME: *Okay, I hear you, Ray. This feels like a good time to recall how to have respectful disagreements. What have we been learning?*

CARLA: *Right—we're supposed to agree or disagree with people's ideas.*

RAY: *And not make it personal.*

ME: *Why?*

CARLA: *Because, we have to be able to respect people's ideas without . . .*

DEANNA: *Because if we don't respect each other, then it won't be a conversation anymore; it'll be a fight, and people will have hurt feelings, and then that will kind of like eat away at our friendships and stuff.*

ME: *Yes, we don't have to agree all the time, but we do need to learn how to disagree respectfully or we won't understand one another's perspective. Remember that we can keep the conversation going by disagreeing with another person's point of view respectfully, but we can shut the conversation down if we start hurting their feelings or making verbal attacks against their character. Do you remember some ways to do this?*

[Students nod and visibly relax from the tension that was seeping into their shared space.]

ME: *As you pick up this conversation again, I'm going to be listening in for that respectful disagreement language you've been practicing, okay?*

[Students nod.]

CARLA: *Okay, I'll start. Ray, I understand that you think Mr. Kline could've grabbed Nick's gun. But I disagree. In a stressful moment like that, I think—like Deanna said—that a person just acts on instinct and not on reason.*

RAY: *Okay, I hear you. I'm just saying that he definitely had the instinct to protect and it seems like—to me—he could've done that better [by] going for the gun.*

KEENAN: *Yeah, I agree with Ray on this. If Mr. Kline had gone for the gun, he'd have saved a lot more lives.*

DEANNA: *I can agree that maybe he would've saved a lot more lives, but I don't agree that he was really able to make that choice in that, like, right when all that was happening. I just don't think he had time to think it out, you know?*

ME: *Okay, pause again. How did that feel compared with the way the conversation was headed before?*

RAY: *Yeah, before, I was thinking it might get ugly and that someone was going to walk away and our discussion would end in a negative way, but this time it felt like we could just keep going and—*

DEANNA: *And nobody had to get defensive. It felt more respectful.*

ME: *Keenan?*

KEENAN: *Yeah, I get it. [Turns to Deanna.] I'm sorry for using the word* stupid *before. I should've just said that it seemed obvious to me and that I didn't understand why it wasn't obvious to you.*

[Deanna smiles.]

Clearly, this group didn't need much more than a reminder of what we'd been practicing before they were able to apply those lessons. Initially, they were conversing as they had (perhaps) always done, but they were able to switch to the more respectful idea-focused language quite quickly. In this way, they had an opportunity to "try on" the language of our course and apply it in an authentic, engaging discussion.

Small-group discussions enable students to push each other's thinking and grow ideas collaboratively, but many teachers have expressed concern that allowing students to talk in small groups simultaneously, as I did in the example above, makes it impossible for the teacher to properly "evaluate" and "assess" the kids' talk. Although it's true that we want to make sure the students are not entrenching themselves in misinformation (Hattie 2012), it is also essential that we give them space for exploratory talk. In his book *Uncommon Sense: Theoretical Practice in Language Education*, John S. Mayher asserts that we simply don't have adequate time to give kids enough opportunity to talk and preside over every conversation for assessment purposes. He suggests that "the solution . . . is to create environments for children to talk with each other in teacherless groups" (1990, 130). When we give our students opportunities to engage in real meaning-making conversations and discussions, we enable them to experience the course content in a way that matches the natural learning process. In such classrooms, "the talk is intended to be one of the major processes through which learning occurs, not merely a way of reporting prior learning" (Mayher 1990, 241).

This can happen in the larger group, too, using something akin to the Harkness method (Phillips Exeter Academy website). In a traditional Harkness setting, twelve students and one teacher gather at an oval table. The students lead a conversation about course content while the teacher participates as both a learner and a facilitator who can nudge them when needed.

Although precious few of us have only twelve students per class, I've found that this method can work in the larger-class setting fairly well. The key is making the expectations clear before students arrive at the conversation "table," which is really the classroom furniture arranged so that all members can sit around a shared center and see each other. Students must come to the discussion prepared to contribute ideas, questions, and problems for the group to explore, and they must be prepared to speak up and listen well.

In my middle grade classes, we used this method toward the ends of units of study, when students had all engaged in many partnership, small-group, and whole-class discussions about the content and were adept at asking open-ended questions, listening respectfully and with an open mind, and building on others' statements to collaboratively construct meaning. It does take some patience and effort to make this sort of arrangement work with a large group of students (I had thirty-two), but if you have the space and a little creativity, it can be very rewarding for all involved.

In his book *Socratic Circles: Fostering Critical and Creative Thinking in Middle and High School*, Matt Copeland (2005) reminds us that when students engage in thoughtful discussions that let them deeply explore curricular content and expand their learning skills, they also engage in "the embracing of a diversity of opinions and perspectives, the broadening of critical thinking, the practice of team-building and community-building strategies, and the tolerance of intricacy and uncertainty" while simultaneously discovering "value and merit in their own voices and ideas" (144).

Further, classroom dialogue with teacher guidance affords students the opportunities to develop their listening skills, respect for others, and—as Jim Heal of Wellington College in England puts it—engage collaboratively in the "imaginative process of learning" (Heal 2014). These developments of effective talk are essential not just to the learning of a particular subject, but also to the cultivation of neurological and political competence. The act of speaking enables our brains to build connections, which is how learning takes hold. Talking helps students become better thinkers and communicators. People who think and communicate well are equipped to engage in social and civic activities. All of this sounds obvious, because it is, and yet student talk remains dreadfully silenced in many of our classrooms.

To be fair, getting students of any age to talk openly and productively, to listen deeply and respond appropriately, requires a great deal of modeling, practicing, and patience. I've had many instances of asking my students to discuss what I considered to be a compelling concept, only to have the room remain silent or fall silent after just a few seconds of timid student speaking. Just the same, there have been countless "conversations" that amounted to little more than kids taking turns to say a little something (often repeating what someone else already said) rather than sharing original ideas, listening carefully, and building on what others had said. These are skills that take time and practice to develop.

Although middle grade students tend to wear their moods on the surface, they can also be guarded, quiet, and intimidated by the spotlight. Asking them to share their ideas about class content, their interpretations, and their opinions can make them feel vulnerable, particularly if they are accustomed to listening to others for the majority of their school day. In my school, students were expected to discuss and collaborate in many classrooms, not just mine. That meant that they were more comfortable with the process than students in other schools might be. They had many chances throughout the day and year to get used to the sounds of their own voices filling the space, the challenge of articulating their ideas and questions to a live audience, the discomfort that comes with disagreements, and the task of revising their ideas in light of new perspectives and information while holding true to their values. My students had been coached in the art of discussion not just by me, but also by their other teachers, and not just for a single year but for all three years they'd spent in our school. Note that the discussion I shared in this chapter was with eighth-grade students. They were in their third year of this highly participatory learning style.

Although it's true that I believe any students of any age in any classroom can learn to use talk effectively in their learning, I also know that the process will take time. As long as we are sensitive and attentive to our students "norms," we can acclimate them to the nuances of discussion, just as we might help them learn how to write a paper or solve a complicated math problem. However, I also believe that, as is true with most things in teaching and learning, we need to tune in to our students, understand what they know and are able to do (and what they are and are not yet comfortable with), and then guide them toward the goal—in this case, meaningful talk that will contribute to their learning and expression. And so, it would be unfair for me to suggest that your students will be highly effective conversationalists within days or even weeks if they are learning to hold peer-to-peer discussions only in your classroom.

The effort is not only worthwhile, but essential to our students' life experiences. How will they seek answers, contribute their ideas, or help improve their world if they never learn how to use their own voices, honor their own ideas, or hear others' perspectives? If we don't give them the space and opportunities to build the skills of conversation, how will they collaborate in the workforce or speak up, whether in favor of things they value or against injustices?

Student talk in our classrooms, then, is much bigger than just a tool for learning our course content (though this is a valuable application). It's a necessary skill for the shaping of our students' lives.

For concrete examples of adding more talk opportunities into your class sessions, see Chapter 3: "The Strategies."

ACTIVE ENGAGEMENT

You've just read a lot about how talk enhances learning. Take a movement break before reading further. Choose an activity that suits you (such as walking, running, jumping, or climbing stairs) and spend five to fifteen minutes doing it.

Then, tell someone about what you've read so far. Explain how talk helps people learn and how you intend to give your students more time for talk in your class. (You might also want to jot down some of those ideas in your plan book or journal.)

If you can't find a partner, try speaking into a recorder (I use my smartphone or computer for this). Later, you can play this back to hear how your thoughts flowed after exercise.

Finally, in your journal, reflect on your experience of the movement and talk. (See Figure 2.3.) How does it affect your ability to process the information you're reading in this book? What effect does it have on your learning?

FIGURE 2.3

An entry from my journal: the power of quick, disruptive talks to solidify learning

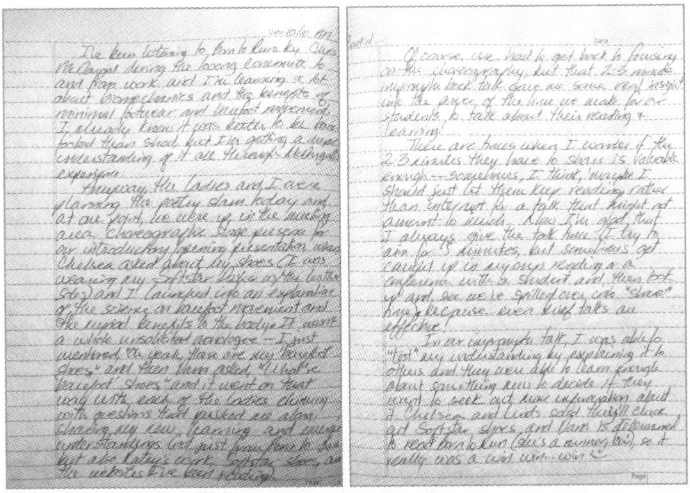

WHY A FLEXIBLE ENVIRONMENT STIMULATES BRAIN ACTIVITY

From our earliest days, we respond to environmental stimulus with profound neurological activity. Research shows that this brain activity continues throughout our lives (it slows to some extent after infancy, but undergoes another surge in adolescence) and that it influences the development of new neural pathways, which is the basis for learning (Jensen and Nutt 2015). Language development, in particular, grows more robust with significant meaningful experiences, such as conversations (even the babbling back and forth between a pre-verbal baby and parent counts here), reading (including when one reads to a pre-verbal child and thereafter), and when a child's utterances prompt responses from other humans.

I think part of the reason kids have such a hard time at this age is because they're not learning in a productive way. If [they] were learning in a creative and active environment, they could be so much more engaged in [their] work and education.
MANON ACHARD, FORMER GRADE 6–8 STUDENT

The same is true for stimuli that affect other areas of the brain, such as those that correlate with the senses and those that influence abstract thinking—such as a painting, or the scent of baking bread—which leads us to believe that increased receptor stimulation improves learning outcomes (Diamond 2001; Van Praag, Kempermann, and Gage 2001).

So what do all of these studies have to do with the classroom environment? In the simplest terms, they show us that we can do more to influence learning in our students' brains than requiring them to sit still and listen to us explain or watch us demonstrate: we can use the often untapped potential of the classroom's physical features.

By introducing a range of environmental stimuli for kids to see, hear, feel, smell, and even taste, we can engage more of their brains in learning tasks, enabling them to "experience" the content on multiple levels. When more of the brain is engaged, research shows, the experience produces more lasting memories and learning is enhanced.

Consider, for example, the difference between reading *Romeo and Juliet* on paper while sitting at a desk in a silent classroom lit by overhead fluorescent lamps, and reading *Romeo and Juliet* on paper while sitting on a beanbag chair in the golden light of a floor-standing reading lamp while sixteenth-century instrumental music gently fills the room. The quality of the sensory experience in the latter example far exceeds the former because the sensory input (the comfortable seating and softer lighting, the melodic sounds in the room) stimulates more parts of the brain. That brain stimulation is then associated with the content of the play, thereby making the experience of the play a richer one, which consequently deems it more memorable than if the student had simply read it with little or harsh sensory input (the hard chair and desk, the bright lighting, the starkness of the silent room). What's more, hearing the music in the future could stimulate the memory of the play even when the learner is not reading the words.

Coming up with effective and creative ways to engage more of our students' brains through environmental shifts can be time consuming, but it becomes easier over time. I began my journey toward creating a richer sensory experience for my students by conferring with my special education colleagues, who led me to a host of methods and modalities such as using tactile manipulatives (think cut-up paper with words and definitions that kids could scatter on the floor and move around to match up, rather than static word and definition lists on a sheet of paper), incorporating soundscapes (like in the *Romeo and Juliet* example above), and visual tools such as images, graphics, and videos, to enhance my lesson plans. These tools naturally lent themselves to using the physical space more purposefully than I had been doing previously. Over time, I learned to get the kids more involved by asking them to choose from a few ideas and then help me create the tools or rearrange the room as needed. Anytime we ask them to help us make decisions, or physically make or move things, our students' brains are more active.

We can also explore the value of periodically altering the classroom decor, adding plant life and even a pet in the room, changing the seating arrangement, and creating new special areas in the classroom to inspire new perspectives. All of these methods help to "wake up" the brains of our students and deepen their learning experiences.

When we add novelty to a class lesson or activity, we cause a response in more parts of the brain than if that experience were nearly identical to previous ones. The human brain reads nearly identical situations as unworthy of significant attention. This translates into kidspeak as "boring." Regardless of which term we use to describe such situations, the fact remains that when less of the brain is stimulated, students exhibit low levels of engagement in the activity, resulting in less-than-stellar learning outcomes. In the middle grades, a wealth of stimuli is vying for our kids' attention, from their budding awareness of one another—they're noticing style, economic and social status, crushes, friendships gained and lost, and more—to their newly sharpened alertness to issues of justice and injustice, so we have to work a bit harder than elementary teachers might to keep their attention on the learning.

Judy Willis, neurologist turned teacher, explains this in terms of our "animal" brain and our more evolved "thinking" brain (TEDx 2013). She says that when the brain is "bored," the higher-thinking modes shut down and the "animal" brain—impulsive, survival driven, reactive—takes over. When this happens, students' brains struggle to attend to the lesson we're teaching, and instead they focus on either finding threatening situations or creating neurological stimulation (usually demonstrated in negative, off-task behaviors). In other words, as Willis explains it, "boredom is a stressor that changes the way the brain works."

Stressed (or bored) brains cannot effectively process new information. For learning to occur, new information needs to be processed through the amygdala to get into the prefrontal cortex. Once there, the information can be further processed into the working memory and finally can be stored in the long-term memory. In stressed brains, though, that information isn't even likely to get through the amygdala.

I'm not saying we need to reinvent the wheel for each lesson, but I am saying that when we get creative (and design ways for kids to be more creative), our students have greater chances of learning more information (see Figures 2.4 and 2.5). I also don't mean to downplay the importance of predictable structures in our classrooms. If students came in to vastly different experiences from one day to the next, their sense of stability and safety would be undermined. Small changes made once or twice in a month or unit of study can have a big effect on learning.

FIGURE 2.4
Many of my classroom charts look like this one, which is a running list of lessons we did throughout a unit of study and serves as a reference for what we've learned so far.

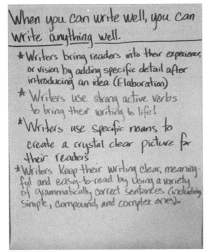

FIGURE 2.5
Because this design is so different from what students are accustomed to seeing in my classroom, it represents enough novelty to catch their attention and evoke some excitement.

Students tend to thrive with some amount of predictability (such as having a consistent workflow—for example, lesson, independent and collaborative work time, whole-class share) and a level of dependability (knowing what to expect from the teacher and what is expected of students) in their classrooms. Within that, though, we can introduce new tools and methods to perk up the brains of our learners and encourage them to engage more deeply in their education. Willis explains why even changing your own behavioral patterns to highlight a new concept is effective. For example, she walks backward to catch the kids' attention when she wants to teach something particularly important. She doesn't do it often, because it would lose its effect, but she has a repertoire of simple tricks that instantly increase students' attention.

ACTIVE ENGAGEMENT

Take three to five minutes to rearrange something in your space (whether you are in your classroom or home writing/work space). Doing something as simple as moving the furniture around, hanging a new piece of art, or adding a large bouquet of fresh flowers can perk up your brain activity in that space.

If you have the time, spend up to five minutes doing something intellectually rigorous in the new space—read something riveting, write a poem, examine a piece of art.

In your journal, reflect on the experience. (See Figure 2.6.) What effect did the physical environment's change have on your psyche? What effect did it have on your attention? How might a similar change in your classroom affect your students?

FIGURE 2.6

An entry from my journal: changing the environment (furniture arrangement) to suit particular curricular needs can have significant effects on learning.

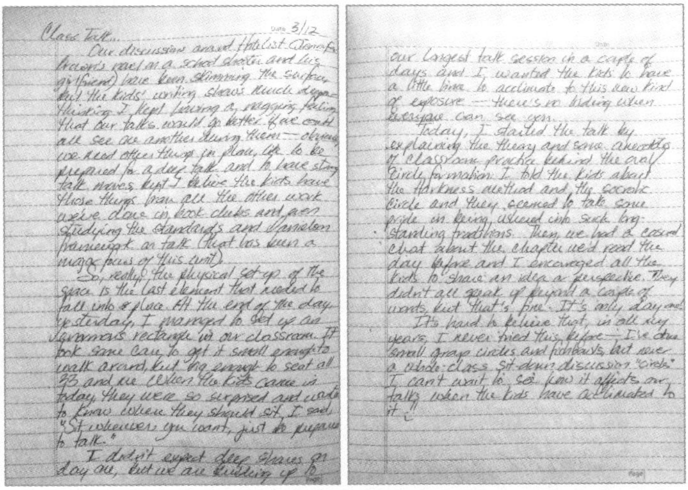

CHAPTER 3

THE STRATEGIES

BEFORE THE LESSON (THE FIRST FIVE MINUTES)

My seventh-grade students have arrived and are lined up outside my classroom door. I don't keep them waiting, but I do like to greet them at the door to set the tone for our class period and remind them that they are entering a space dedicated to work and cooperation.

I open the door and smile at the group.

"Welcome back! It's so good to see you all again," I say. "Go ahead inside and follow the 'Do Now' instructions, please." (See Figure 3.1.)

As they enter, I make eye contact with each of them and repeat my welcome message a few times to ensure everyone has heard it. Following the last student into the room, I close the door and enjoy the purposeful chatter. Some students are already paired up and walking around the room as they talk. The students are doing exactly what they've been instructed to do.

The "Do Now" says this:

- While standing, unpack and consider the following statements:

    A) The "essay" is an academic genre that doesn't exist outside of school.

    B) Essays are used frequently in the world—not just in schools— and are found in all types of publications.

- *While walking around the room with your partner, discuss these two statements. Explain which you believe is true and why.*
  - *Circle the room twice, and then come to the meeting area with ELA materials.*

FIGURE 3.1

We often think start-of-class activities need be purely intellectual, but adding movement and student talk to these tasks engages more of the brain while making the learning space feel more dynamic than if kids went directly to their seats for silent work.

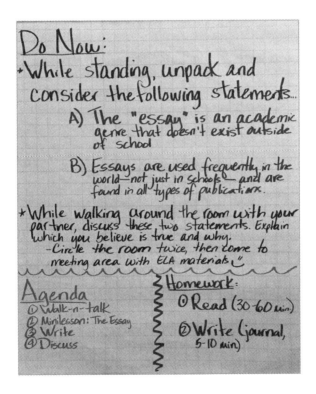

As the students walk and talk, I ensure that all of my lesson materials are at my teaching station and listen to their chatter as they pass by. I'll use what I hear to lead into my lesson today. It pleases me immensely that they take the task seriously and

share some compelling insights that help me understand what they already know—and think they know—about the genre we're launching into.

After two or three minutes, the students make their way to the meeting area and await the lesson.

We all know that the first five minutes of a class session can have a powerful effect on the way the period plays out, so we are careful to set the intention of productivity right away. We want our students' time to add value to their learning.

Starting a class with movement and talk accomplishes this and more. Not only are we setting the tone for focus and productivity by orchestrating an activity that pulls students into the content of the class by engaging their prior knowledge, experience, and thoughts on the topic that will be addressed in the lesson, but we're also providing the oxygenation—which we learned about in Chapter 2—their brains need to function at optimal levels.

There's another benefit to this kind of activity that contributes deeply to the learning process: talking with peers allows students to practice having collegial conversations. These talks are essential opportunities to articulate coherent thought, listen carefully, consider a peer's perspective, and build ideas together. As mentioned in Chapter 2, talking and listening in this way has a far greater effect on learning than just reading or listening to a teacher explain concepts.

When we consider the first five minutes of our class sessions, there are a lot of variables to take into account. For example, perhaps you already use that time for "warm-up" activities or you believe that quiet independent work is a better way to set the tone for the class period. Keep in mind that the first five minutes is only one place to incorporate movement and talk into your class session. Another thing to consider is your goal and purpose for the work you provide to students when they first arrive in your class. If the purpose is to prepare them for deep engagement in learning tasks, then you might want to consider building some movement and talk into these early activities.

THE FIRST TIME: PROVIDING CLEAR INSTRUCTION AND EXPECTATIONS

If you've never instructed your students to walk and talk before and you're concerned about confusion or off-task behavior, then the following tips will be helpful.

Our students want to know why we make the choices we make about their education. What's more, middle school students are developing their inner sense of rationalizing: they want to be better informed, and to take part in some decision making. I believe that being open with them about our motivations is important in a number of ways, not the least of which is that it affirms the trust they place in us. When we're open and honest, our students appreciate it and are more inclined to follow us into new experiences.

For this reason, it makes sense, any time we are going to try something new in the classroom, to let the students know why we want to do it. For one thing, giving a scientifically validated reason is far more convincing and motivating to students than any version of "It's good for you," or "Remember, I'm grading you on participation."

Another reason to share the research that drives our choices in how we run our classes is that it encourages student independence. When we explain that our research has led us to make important decisions about how we conduct our own lives and our classroom teaching practices, we show students that research doesn't stop being relevant when we graduate from school; rather, it is an important part of life. This inspires them to research things that interest them outside of school.

In this way, we also alert our students to the fact that the research about learning is ongoing and we are wise to continue following and applying it, wherever possible, to enhance our learning experiences and our lives.

Therefore, I recommend that you chat with your students before asking them to engage in new learning behaviors, such as walking around the room while talking about a specific topic with a peer. Your talk could go something like this:

ACTIVATE

*Recently, I learned that moving our bodies
helps our brains work better.*

*Research shows that movement encourages
the brain to focus on information and the
kinds of learning tasks you encounter all
day long in school. We also know that it's
important for learners to have opportunities to
talk about what they're learning.*

*So today, I'd like us to try something a little
different. I'm going to ask you to walk around
the room with your partner and have a brief
discussion about today's topic. I'll do this with
you, because I know it can help me just as
much as it can help you.*

*I wouldn't ask you to do something if I didn't
believe it was going to improve your learning
experiences, and I look forward to seeing
how this works. I'll leave time at the end of
the period for us to talk about how the new
activity felt for you this first time around.*

*Before we start walking, I'd like to be clear
about safety. Though you'll be talking
while you walk, please be alert to your
surroundings, and avoid bumping into or*

tripping over things or each other. We'll
all walk in the same direction and at a
comfortable, slow pace. No speed walking.

Did I leave anything out? [Allow students to
suggest other safety guidelines.]

Great. I'm going to set a timer for two
minutes. That should be long enough for you
and your partner to each share one idea and
respond to each other. Our topic is posted
[indicate where in the room]. Let's all read it
before we start our walk. [After everyone has
read the prompt, ask if there are any questions
and then proceed with the timed activity.]

Doing the activity with your students the first two or three times (and randomly thereafter) will give you invaluable insight. You'll experience how it feels to do this work and understand whether the length of time is adequate, you are able to focus on the content prompt while walking, and the pace you've requested is too slow or fast. You'll also get a keener perspective on the layout of your room, noticing which areas need a little reorganization to improve the safety and flow for walking students.

An added bonus to participating alongside your students is that you communicate the undeniable message that what's good for them is good for you, further increasing their motivation to participate.

Like Alan Sitomer, a three-time teacher of the year reminds us, "Do as I say, not as I do" is never a good approach in the classroom (Sitomer 2008). If we always instruct students to do tasks they never see us engage in, they glean that we consider ourselves to be "other" than them. Creating a sense of unity in the classroom means sometimes doing the very tasks we ask our students to do, including the worksheets and writing we ask them to complete. Of course, this also keeps us highly in tune with the skills our students need to apply to succeed in our classes.

VARIATIONS

Once you've tried the pre-lesson walk-and-talk, you can get creative about using movement and discussion in a variety of ways at the start of class. Here are a few other ideas to get you started:

- Have students do twenty jumping jacks, then stand at their desks or tables while unpacking, before convening for your lesson.

- Ask students to briefly discuss what they recall from the previous day's study (or homework), while standing, just before settling in for your lesson.

- Do a timed mingle: on their feet, kids find a partner and talk for two minutes about a topic. At the end of two minutes (signaled by a timer), they find another partner and talk for another two minutes. Students can meet with three different partners and then convene for whole-class sharing of ideas that came up.

- Start class with silent, reflective, nonstop writing (students can write to a prompt linked to the topic of the day or unit) for three minutes. At the end, students can walk and talk to share and discuss their ideas for two minutes.

No doubt you'll find myriad ways to incorporate movement and talk in the first five minutes of class sessions. The key to making these strategies maximize learning is to link the content of the activities to the content of the course or day's lesson. This is an effective way to get your students to activate their thinking about course content while priming their brains for more information on the same topics.

ACTIVE ENGAGEMENT

Do you have a lesson-planning session scheduled with a coteacher or colleague? Suggest you spend the first few minutes of that meeting in a walk-and-talk. Get your big ideas flowing in conversation while walking around (outdoors, if you can, to absorb some natural daylight), then return to your books and computers to map out your plans more concretely.

If you don't have a planning session scheduled within the next few hours, then try doing this at home with a family member. Instead of talking about lesson plans, talk about what to make for dinner or share big ideas for a family vacation or fun day. When you get back from your walk, put your ideas down on paper or a digital document and turn them into a plan.

Then, grab your journal to reflect. (See Figure 3.2.) Describe the effects of your walk-and-talk and answer the question "How can this experience better inform my classroom instruction practices?"

FIGURE 3.2

An entry from my journal: the power of a pre-meeting walk with colleague

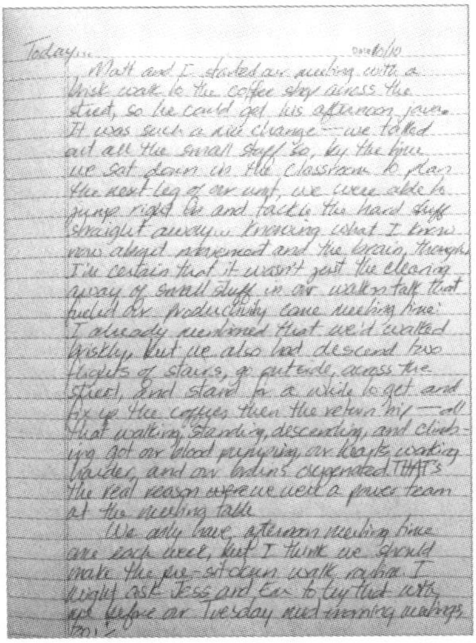

Today... Date 6/10

Matt and I started our meeting with a brisk walk to the coffee shop across the street, so he could get his afternoon java. It was such a nice change—we talked out all the small stuff so, by the time we sat down in the classroom to plan the next leg of our unit, we were able to jump right in and tackle the hard stuff straight away... Knowing what I know now about movement and the brain, though, I'm certain that it wasn't just the clearing away of small stuff in our walk-n-talk that fueled our productivity come meeting time: I already mentioned that we'd walked briskly, but we also had descend two flights of stairs, go outside, across the street, and stand for a while to get and fix up the coffee, then the return trip—all that walking, standing, descending, and climbing got our blood pumping, our hearts working harder, and our brains oxygenated. THAT'S the real reason we were a power team at the meeting table.

We only have afternoon meeting time once each week, but I think we should make the pre-sitdown walk regular. I might ask Jess and Em to try that with us before our Tuesday mid-morning meetings too!

DURING THE LESSON

It's our second day reading an excerpt from Jim Murphy's The Great Fire *as we work through Laura Robb's unit on Reading Informational Texts (Robb 2013). In just a few minutes, the students are meant to be discussing the informational-genre characteristics they can identify in the excerpt. I've projected the text onto our screen so everyone can see and refer to it. Rather than direct the students to our meeting area, I had them go directly to their seats at the start of class, where they'll begin their partner work momentarily.*

For today's session, I'm not really teaching a lesson; I'm just getting the kids set up for their work by reminding them about the text (we read it yesterday) and some characteristics of the informational genre. As I talk, I look into their faces and make eye contact with each of them. I can't help but notice how lethargic they look. We've been together only a few minutes, but it's near the end of the school day, and they appear tired and mentally drained.

To check in with their attention, I say, "As we read this article on the blizzard again today, you'll be looking for the poetic elements and characteristics," emphasizing the words blizzard *and* poetic, *hoping they catch on that I failed to say* fire *and* genre. *No response. Not even a head tilt. They are not with me. None of my words are registering.*

"Okay," I say, "it's clear that we need to move these bodies to wake up these brains. Stand up and push in your chair, please." I ignore the groans as I swiftly walk to my desk and pick up my phone. "We'll dance-walk for the length of one song," I say, and as the words are leaving my mouth, I hand the phone to Angelica and motion for her to choose a song from the playlist I've pulled up. "We'll move in this direction first," I say as I gesture with my arm. "Listen for my signal for when to change," and the phone is in the speaker stand. "Have fun, everyone, and get that body moving!"

Angelica's chosen a fairly popular song (Taylor Swift's "You Belong with Me") and some of the kids start hopping and giggling and grabbing their friends' arms. Everyone is moving. Some started out by shuffling lazily along, but they're starting to liven up now.

I move with the group, going slightly faster than them so I can cheer them on and then move along to the next little cluster of kids to do the same. I'm hopping and skipping, jogging, and walking fast. It feels really good. The music is upbeat, and some of the kids are singing along, which makes me happy. I keep working my way around so I can see every student and each of them can see me. We smile at one another, and I clap joyfully and remind the really excited kids to land softly as they jump, so as not to pound on the floor and disturb our neighbors downstairs or next door.

About halfway through the song, I get into the middle of the room and sweep my arm to indicate it's time to change directions, and the crowd reverses its path.

By the time the song ends, most of us are panting and everyone is visibly perked up. I turn off the music and tell everyone to remain standing in a circle facing its center. "David, please lead us through some stretches," I say, taking a space in the circle line.

David leads us through leg, arm, and torso stretches the students are familiar with from physical education class.

When he's through, everyone instinctively applauds him as he makes his way back into the circle. I say, "Thank you for leading us, David, and thank you, everyone, for having a dance with me. That was fun! Now, when you get back to your seats, you'll be working through this text on the Chicago fire, which we read yesterday, and you'll be finding and discussing informational genre elements in that text. Here [I indicate the chart shown in Figure 3.3] is our list of some of the characteristics of informational texts that you can refer to throughout this work. Are there any questions before we start?"

Amanda raises her hand and asks, "Should we write down . . . like, the parts that we find?"

"Oh, thank you for asking that, Amanda. Since you'll have a copy of the text in front of you for this work, you'll want to use those annotating techniques we've practiced, to indicate where you find the characteristics in the text. Does that make sense?"

Maria says, "So, we should maybe list the characteristics in the margins, but, like, underline or highlight the sentences?"

"That sounds good. What do the rest of you think about that idea?"

Heads nod in general agreement.

"What can you do besides underline and highlight?"

"Ooh," Henry offers, "we can use that thing that shows, um, when there's like a big part that has it . . ."

"Does anyone know what Henry means?" I ask.

"Oh, brackets," Milo says.

"Brackets, yes, thank you, Henry and Milo. Brackets are another great tool for annotating. Anything else before we get started?"

The kids are quiet but attentive. They look like they're ready to get into the work.

"Great," I say. "I'll be coming around to see how it goes." And off they scuttle to their seats, all traces of the earlier lethargy utterly erased from their demeanors.

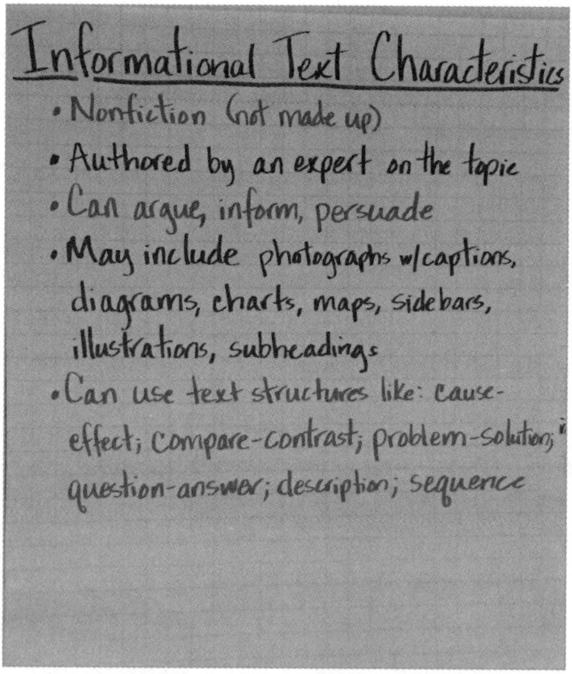

FIGURE 3.3
As students learn to identify, analyze, and create informational-text characteristics, I keep a chart like this on the wall for reference.

ADDING MOVEMENT TO THE MIX

Sometimes, we need to offer fairly rigorous movement at the start of our class periods, as I did in the preceding scenario. Simply tuning in to our students' energy levels and responsiveness is all we need do to know when such a break is necessary. Had only one to three students been showing signs of sluggish-brain syndrome, I'd have offered those students the opportunity to walk around the room, go get water, or do some jumping jacks to get focused as the rest of the class carried on through the instructions from their seats. There will certainly be times, though, when the majority of students are in a slump and classroom productivity demands a movement break.

This can happen during a lesson, too. Occasionally, we teach lessons that extend beyond the coveted ten-minute time frame we know is ideal for adolescent attention spans.

During longer lessons, we do well to add some movement to the students' engagement. The simplest and least time-consuming way is to have students stand in place throughout the turn-and-talk and whole-class share (if you decide to do these activities). You can get creative about adding movement by trying a variety of methods. Having a repertoire of "moves" to choose from enables you to keep things interesting for your students and to assign different activities for different purposes and effects.

Here are a few ideas to get you started:

> Walkie Talkie: Break midway through a long lesson for a two-minute walk-and-talk (see "Before the Lesson [The First Five Minutes]" for description). Be sure to direct students to talk about what's been taught and how it fits with what they've learned previously, and to articulate any questions they're formulating at this point in the lesson or unit of study.

> Move It!: Pause the lesson and lead students through a quick exercise of twenty jumping jacks and a few careful stretches with deep breaths, then get back to teaching.

Jumping jacks not your thing? How about Simon Says? Or jogging in place?

Scavengers, Engage: Include a brief scavenger hunt for items pertaining to your lesson that you've planted around the room. Tell students what to find (with drawings on the board, perhaps?) and have students seek out the items and bring them up to your "stage" for the demonstration part of your lesson.

The Outfield: Take part of your lesson outdoors. Teach one part of the lesson in the classroom, and then lead the students outside for the remainder of the lesson. The transition walk will do wonders for their attention and energy.

Zone Shift: Move the class to a different part of the room for the second half of the lesson and instruct the kids to talk about what's been taught so far as they transition.

Game Time: When eyes begin to glaze over, have your students stand, face a partner, and engage in a quick hand game, such as Rock, Paper, Scissors or Miss Mary Mack, then sit back down for the remainder of your lesson.

Pop Quiz Catch: Create an impromptu quiz on the content from the first half of your lesson. Have students stand and spread apart, forming a circle with you included. Use a small ball or other soft object and toss it from one student to another, asking questions along the way. Whoever catches the ball or object needs to answer the question. Increase willingness to participate by making this low stakes: wrong answers are opportunities to correct misunderstandings.

Standing Room Only: Have students stand facing you, preferably in a semicircle so you can see each face and each student can see you. Resume your lesson in this formation, and then let students sit again after five minutes or so.

Stand, If You Please: Offer students the option to stand at any point during your lesson, so long as it is not disruptive to collective focus. Be sure to have standing zones set up in your room so that standing students don't block the view of seated ones. When they realize their brains are growing lethargic, students can quietly move to a standing zone and you never have to miss a beat.

PARTNER TALKS

Many of us aim to keep our lessons brief, knowing that our students' attention span wanes after ten minutes or so. We also want to make sure kids have plenty of time to engage with the material directly, building experiential knowledge and skills. On days when a lesson lasts only up to ten minutes, students will benefit from peer talk sessions but are not likely to need a movement break to jog their brains back into full-fledged functioning mode. During longer lessons, however, we'll want to incorporate some form of moving into the peer talk breaks.

A simple turn-and-talk or T&T, as many literacy teachers refer to this method, is enough to engage students in authentic active processing of lesson content. These brief talk breaks can be easily incorporated into brief lessons, as well as longer lessons, and need last only a minute or two. At its most basic, this is when students turn to face a peer and talk about whatever the prompt is—usually something the teacher has just taught or described—or whatever the students are wondering about regarding the lesson. Students can talk in pairs or in small groups, for brief or extended periods of time. Talk is a powerful tool in the learning process, as discussed in Chapter 2 of this book.

During a lesson, pausing now and then to let kids quickly talk about what they're seeing or hearing, or even what they are confused about, helps them actively incorporate the new content or skill into their working memories. It also enables them to determine the level of their understanding, preparing them for self-directed follow-up steps, such as paying closer attention during the rest of your lesson or articulating specific questions for further support. Since middle schoolers are developmentally ready to contribute more to their learning, this practice effectively trains them to acknowledge their thoughts about what we are teaching and to more fully formulate those thoughts by articulating and sharing them.

Breaking up our lessons with partner talks also serves to keep kids attentive. When they are required to sit, watch, and listen for ten minutes or more at a stretch, their minds tend to wander away from what we want them to focus on. What's more, even if they are able to follow along without distraction, taking in that much material is bound to result in minimal retention if we don't interrupt the "intake" for active mental processing. Talking with a partner requires cogitation, but it also provides a buffer of space in the flow of information from the teacher. Within that buffer, students can process the content and incorporate it into their working memories.

It's valuable to keep talks brief during a lesson. If our kids are talking in pairs, then one to two minutes is often long enough. Groups need a little more time for each partner to share, which is why you'll want to keep group size to a minimum during lessons. Each partner gets thirty to sixty seconds to speak, and neither one has enough time to change the topic or wander off task.

Here's an example of how this played out in one of my eighth-grade lessons:

[Approximately four minutes into the lesson] So far, I've described for you the purpose of an application essay and we looked at one example. Turn to your partner and say what you are noticing about this type of writing.

[I listen for key phrases and nod as I scan each partnership one after the other, showing kids that I hear what they're saying. I observe the whole group to see that everyone is engaged. After about a minute, I start speaking.]

Tip: This is an invaluable lesson I learned from Mary Ehrenworth at the Teachers College Reading and Writing Project. It has served me and my students well for years! Because I don't want to spend time waiting for everyone's attention—

and risk extending my lesson so long that I sacrifice the kids' work time—I start talking (when I want the kids' talks to end) and don't stop. Soon the kids catch on that I'm not going to wait for them and they end their conversations. The key here is that I start my speech with refocusing phrases so that no one misses important information. The following demonstrates how I've done this.

Thank you, writers. [Many students instantly look to me and stop talking at the sound of my voice, because they're accustomed to this tactic at this point in the school year.] I'm impressed with how quickly you got into your shares just now [by now only two or three partnerships are still talking] and I could hear that you picked up on some key [now I have everyone's attention] elements of the application essay. [Now I'll share the important information I need them to get from the rest of the lesson.]

Consider inserting partner talk time after key points in your teaching by saying, "I just gave you a lot of information. Turn and talk to the person next to you about what you heard me say." Stop them after thirty or forty-five seconds. At this point, you may choose to simply go on with your lesson, or you may decide that it would be valuable to share some of what was said in those brief partner talks. If you do decide to share, you'll want to be mindful of the time and share in the most efficient way. Sometimes that'll mean asking a student to repeat something you overheard in the share, and other times it'll mean simply paraphrasing what you heard (or what you wanted or expected to hear).

Tip: Perhaps you expected to hear kids say they noticed something specific about the content of your lesson but you didn't actually hear anybody say it. You can say, "I'm pretty sure I heard a couple of you say something really smart. You said [important specific message]. . . ." This way, the kids feel validated for their work and engagement but they also hear the important information you didn't want them to miss. Just be careful to do this only occasionally, or the kids will catch on and assume that you aren't really listening when they talk. Most often, you will hear what you hope they've been learning and can honestly share that with the whole group. You'll also want to share other valid tidbits the kids came up with on their own.

Using partner talks will increase the learning outcomes in your classroom if you haven't been using them already. Keep in mind, the point isn't that you always hear what each pair shares, but that they have the opportunity to "try the content on," so to speak, in their own voices and words, so they can get clear about what they do and do not understand. Talking, like writing, enables the kids to effectively build up their working memory with the content you are teaching.

OTHER WAYS TO INCORPORATE PARTNER TALK DURING LESSONS

If interrupting your lessons for kids to verbalize their learning doesn't feel doable, then you might consider these other options as more viable solutions in your classroom:

- Before your lesson, tell kids the topic of the lesson and let them talk with partners for one to two minutes to generate some predictions or questions about what's to come or to access prior knowledge on the subject.

- At the end of your lesson, before students get into independent or group work, allow two or three minutes for peer talk about the lesson. Include a whole-class share at the end to benefit everyone's emerging understanding. You might also consider taking just another minute or so for a quick Q&A, which is sure to clear up some confusion and provide you with an assessment of their comprehension of the material.

- Allow kids to talk as needed during their work session after your lesson. They can discuss the content and raise questions for one another as you circulate the room and offer support.

- Direct students to T&T midway through their work session, to ensure all are on the right track, and take a moment to address any questions that have come up for them.

- As the students work, circulate the room and check in with partners, groups, or clusters of students, asking them to explain to you what they're doing, why they're doing it, what they've learned, what questions they have, and so on.

One thing to keep in mind is that using brief bouts of movement and talk throughout the class period, rather than implementing them after learning and work times are over, is most beneficial for student learning. Of course, there are learning tasks that require long bouts of silence and stillness (see "Master Class" and the section called "Movement and High-Stakes Tests" in Chapter 5), during which these methods would not be appropriate. In those cases, giving the kids movement and talk time before the long session begins will optimize their energy and attention for the task.

ACTIVE ENGAGEMENT

Find someone to talk to right now. Tell them about what you just read, and explain, in your own words, one or two of the concepts or strategies outlined in this chapter. Share the questions that are coming up for you, and invite your conversation partner to ask questions, too, if any come up for him or her as you talk.

Next, take two to three minutes to write in your journal about how you think talking about this material while it was still quite fresh in your mind may have helped you process it more deeply. Include how or when you can give your students a similar opportunity during your next class session.

AFTER THE LESSON (STUDENTS AT WORK, TEACHER AS COACH)

Our lesson on monitoring for meaning while reading informational texts (see Figure 3.4) is wrapping up, and my sixth-grade students are still in the meeting area, making a plan for their independent reading work before I dismiss them to their seats.

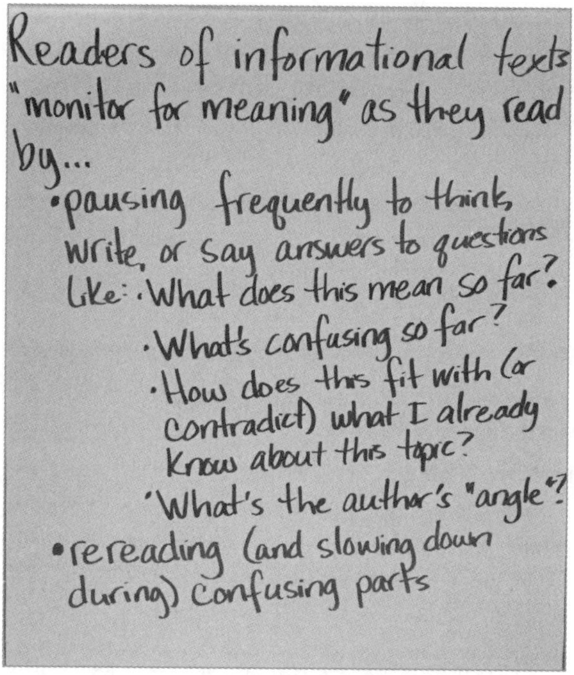

FIGURE 3.4

This classroom chart shows two ways readers monitor for meaning when reading informational texts.

I lean in to a cluster of students who've indicated that their plans are intact and they're ready to get to work. At my signal (a silent thumbs-up) they quietly scurry off to their seats and prepare their work spaces, laying out their texts, notebooks, sticky notes, and pens or pencils. The next group gets my signal, and soon all students are quietly reading at their tables.

I spend a few moments organizing my own materials, collecting my conference notes clipboard, my pen, and my reading notebook in case someone will benefit from seeing my notes. This time also allows my students a chance to get fully focused on their work before I start circulating the room. If I begin too soon, readers don't have enough time to immerse themselves in the work and my footsteps will prevent them from finding that focus.

When I sense the weight of deep reading in the air, I begin my very quiet circulation, peeking at my students' work, reading what they jot on their sticky notes or notebook pages, noticing who is or isn't coming up for air, noticing who is or isn't trying the strategy I just taught them (writing brief notes, showing their work of tracking meaning, throughout the reading of the text).

Before moving on from one table, where all the students have paused reading to jot a note about the content of their text, I lean in to quickly assess their attempts. Three students get a teeny smiley face on their paper, a symbol of my approval of their effort and execution. Two others get a question mark from me, indicating that their note doesn't yet demonstrate the strategy I asked them to try (they know how to interpret my symbols, because we've gone over this and have a chart of them on the wall for reference), and I whisper, "Keep going—I'll be back."

By the time I've made my way around to see everyone's early attempts at this new strategy, I've noted on my clipboard that there are five students I want to see about putting the strategy into practice (because I saw no evidence of that effort the first time around), three to whom I want to reteach the strategy (because they clearly tried, but missed the mark), and a few students I want to revisit to see if their subsequent attempts are as successful as their first.

To begin my conferences, I tap the shoulders of kids who need the strategy retaught and ask them to bring their texts and notes to the meeting area of our classroom (a carpeted space). When we convene there, I say, "I was glad to see each of you try the strategy I just taught in today's lesson. I noticed that your first attempt didn't get at the meaning of the text yet, so we're gathered here to ensure that your next attempts do. You'll remember that in the lesson, we talked about the difference between writing what the text says—but in our own words—and writing our own thoughts about it. They are not the same thing. Although our thoughts about what *we're reading are valuable, they aren't what we're getting after in this particular strategy. This strategy helps us first understand what the text is teaching us, so our notes should reflect what the text actually says. Let's try this together, okay? I'm going to read a paragraph and each of you will write, in just a few words, what the paragraph says. Remember, we are not writing what we think about the paragraph. Everybody got that?" The students nod and lean in to listen as I read aloud a brief paragraph about Ho Chi Minh's role in the Vietnam War. When I reach the end of the paragraph, the students write their single-sentence summary of the text.*

When I read their notes, one by one, I offer feedback.

"Jack, this one says what this section of text was about. Well done. What was different for you this time compared with when you were writing about your own book at your table seat?"

"This time," Jack says, "I just focused on the words in the paragraph, not the words in my mind—not my thoughts."

"How about you, Terri? What helped you this time around?"

"I just think I was confused before, but when you explained it this time, it made more sense to me."

One of the group members holds back his note and says, "Oh, wait, I need to fix this."

I wait until he finishes his writing and then he shows me what he's done. As I read, he explains, "I did it wrong, but now I fixed it and it shows what the paragraph was about."

"Okay, so tell me how you realized you hadn't done the strategy yet."

"Well, just hearing you and Terri helped me realize that I still had work to do."

"I see. Good for you, Sayid, for listening in and figuring that out for yourself," I say. Then addressing the whole group, I add, "Are you all feeling more confident now about monitoring the text's meaning as you read?"

When the students indicate that they are confident now, I instruct them to silently read the next paragraph in our shared text on Ho Chi Minh and to write a single-sentence summary of that paragraph. They do this successfully, so I high-five each of them and send them off to continue their independent work.

This scenario demonstrates a coaching style of teaching and incorporates the concepts of movement and talk to enhance learning. Notice how, immediately after the lesson, I gave students time and space to independently try the skill taught in that lesson. During this independent practice, I closely observed their efforts and offered direct, immediate feedback to each student, spending more time with those who had not fully grasped the lesson from the start.

Identifying a small group of students who needed further instruction, I then provided a mini–movement break by having them get up from their seats and walk to a different spot in the room where they sat on the floor (the different seated posture benefits the body and brain). Katy Bowman, biomechanist and author, encourages variety in posture throughout the day to keep the brain functioning optimally and to prevent underuse and stiffness in muscles, joints, and bones (Bowman 2014).

Next, I briefly retaught the lesson, let the students practice with support (reading the text aloud aided comprehension of the text, so students could focus their attention on the strategy of summarizing it) and, again, provided immediate feedback, including questions that allowed the students to articulate the thinking behind their attempts—which is where I incorporated student talk into the task. Finally, I had the students apply the skill with no support (students read silently and wrote their samples without discussion). When I was convinced the students were on the right track, I sent them back to their independent work spaces for continued application of the skill.

This "coaching" method mimics the way my tennis and basketball coaches worked with me. Their demonstration of the skill, close observation of my initial attempts, and immediate feedback helped me get the moves right early on, so I could practice effectively and strengthen my skills over time. We often hear that teachers have a lot to learn from sports coaches, and I believe this is what people mean by that.

TEACHER AS COACH

Though more than a century has passed since John Dewey and his peers pioneered the concepts of progressive education, including the ideal that learning happens in hands-on experiences (Dewey 2015), realizing those ideals continues to be a challenge. We've grown to acknowledge that there are many pathways to learning and a multitude of methods that different people respond to, but I believe in the fundamental notion that learning through experience is, for most people, far more effective than learning through passive means. Neuroscience shows us that different parts of the brain engage when there are multiple points of sensory input within a given experience. When different parts of the brain engage for a singular task, that experience registers more significantly in the working memory, and later in long-term memory, so students who actively engage in multisensory learning experiences enjoy meaningful and lasting learning outcomes (Jensen and Nutt 2015).

Orchestrating effective active engagement in the classroom requires us to shift our role from "sage" during a lesson to coach during student work time. Teachers become chief feedback coaches who can help students hone their skills and understanding until they demonstrate proficiency. Once proficient, students can continue applying their knowledge and skills in myriad ways until they reach mastery. Students will use these newly developed abilities and understandings in real problems or situations, creating original applications for the learned concepts or when teaching what they've learned to others. Along the way, it's the students who are doing most of the work, engaging in more of the talk, and figuring out how to handle the challenges that arise while the teacher serves as a guide, a sounding board, a support. For this to happen, at some point the teacher has to stop teaching and let the kids start engaging their minds, hands, and voices. In their book *Who's Doing the Work? How to Say Less So Readers Can Do More* (2016), Jan Burkins and Kim Yaris remind us, "When children inhabit worlds where their teachers let them do the work, they learn from their productive effort, become empowered to take charge of their reading lives, and, very often, surprise us with what they can do!" (144).

Stepping down from the pulpit does call upon teachers to acquire and sharpen new skills. Frankly, I think that this is when teaching becomes more interesting. Just like our students, when we are challenged appropriately and in meaningful ways, we too "wake up" with increased interest and investment in our work. And what could be more meaningful to educators than ensuring that each of their students is assimilating into his or her working repertoire the concepts, skills, and information we are teaching them?

The teacher-as-coach concept challenges us to engage deeply in the whole gamut of teaching skills. We'll need to watch, listen, and assess on our feet (literally, in most cases). We'll need to quickly find solutions to the many problems students will demonstrate as they approximate what they're learning, and we'll need to offer guidance in the moment without overtaking the kids with too much talk or too invasive a demonstration—meaning without robbing them of the chance to "do" the work of learning. At first, it may feel clunky and stressful, but over time, with practice, it will smooth out and we and our students will be grateful for the change. In this model, the students' learning is enhanced by increased brain activity inherent in active engagement, and the results will far outweigh results earned from silent, still students who listen to lectures and fill in worksheets.

Serving as a coach in classroom learning experiences requires us to learn when to stop talking and when to let students fumble, if that's what they need, toward understanding. It forces us to do as Laura Robb often urges: "Give [your students] a chance to surprise you." We have to let go of our limited expectations of students' abilities and interest levels, because when they are given the space in which to activate their brains and the encouragement to try—even when they have no confidence in their ability or knowledge yet—then they can surprise us. What's more, they can surprise themselves.

When our students surprise themselves by experiencing a breakthrough or accomplishing something they'd doubted they could, they allow themselves to imagine more surprises, more possibilities for their own growth. This is how motivation is born.

This is how kids become interested in something new. It's how intrinsic reward is realized. When this happens, our classrooms liven up with excitement, and kids are animated with new hope. In this way, we "wake up" the energy in our classrooms and enliven course content in the process. In this way, we deepen the learning experiences of our students.

ACTIVE ENGAGEMENT

Prepare your brain for learning by getting physically active for five to twenty minutes.

Ask someone nearby to teach you something. It can be a friend, partner, or child. Everybody has something to teach. It should be something they can teach inside of five minutes—how to open an orange differently from how you do, how to log on to a video game you've never played and choose your avatar, how to draw a funny face. The key is for someone to teach you something you don't already know how to do. (In other words, don't fake it.)

Ask the "teacher" to watch you try and offer feedback directly after having explained and/or demonstrated the skill. Pay close attention to how it feels to receive feedback during this vulnerable time of trying something new. Notice how you respond as a learner: Do you ask clarifying questions? Do you want to fumble through on your own until you get a feel for the task? Do you want your teacher to do all the work for you? Do you communicate to your teacher when you feel confident enough to do the task independently?

In your journal, write to explore the different ways this could have gone: Could your teacher have been more understanding? Could you have been more willing to accept feedback on your technique? What would've happened if your teacher had given no feedback at all? Do you think you would have reached proficiency in the skill as quickly?

Next, reflect on how this experience informs your classroom practice with students.

CHAPTER 4

THE SPACE

THE FIRST THREE WEEKS

It's the end of our first full week together, and I'm sitting at my desk after all the students have left the building, considering partnership and seat assignments for Monday morning. This week, I instructed the students to choose a different seat near new peers each day, but now I want to settle them into a more formalized arrangement that will last for a few days, if not the whole week.

While looking at my students' names and thinking about all I've learned about them so far, which—with ninety-two students—is understandably minimal, I decide to pair them randomly, making an effort to keep girls with girls and boys with boys. That'll change later on, but early in the year, middle school kids tend to prefer to talk with peers of the same sex. Next, I take out my classroom floor plan and put the names into place, trying to imagine how the pairs will support the other partnerships seated at the same table. (We don't have individual desks in my school; long before I arrived, our administrators furnished the classrooms with six-foot-long tables to encourage collaboration).

When all the kids have been assigned a space on paper, I take a moment to consider how I'll get them into their new seats and talking with their new partners at the start of our very next class session without using up so much time that it eats into instruction. After considering a few possibilities, I decide to quickly craft name-card table tents, using those huge index cards that I could never find a purpose for, and place them in the appropriate places for my first-period class on Monday. I organize the other name tents by table and put a rubber band around them so they're ready for the short transition between class periods.

71

This way, students can go right to their new seats and get ready for class without wasting a single moment. Next, I'll have them talk with their new partners about their personal experiences with listening to talk radio. This connects to my lesson, which will include listening to an excerpt from a National Public Radio story, reading the transcript, and discussing the story elements. This new-partner talk will last just two to three minutes before I gather everyone in the meeting area for the whole-class lesson.

Since we practiced how to enter the classroom and unpack quickly, where to find the instructions for immediate work ("Do Now" or "Bell Work"), and how to get that work done in just a few moments, and since the kids have had a lot of practice already with finding new seats and new talk partners, I'm confident that this plan will run quite smoothly and we will not lose any precious instructional minutes getting acquainted with new seats or partners.

Setting up structures and expectations early in the school year offers monthslong benefits. Our students are paying close attention to everything we do, say, and ask of them during this period, because they want to know what to expect when they walk in the door each day. They also want to know what is expected of them. Their attention is primed and searching for patterns of predictability. If we want to use movement and peer-to-peer talk in the classroom to enhance their cognitive functions throughout the year, then starting this work right away allows students to recognize movement and discussion as predictable components of their class work.

Usually when I talk about getting kids up and moving about the room early in the school year, teachers look at me anxiously, which is understandable. We tend to think first of the potential *problems* with mobility in the classroom, and then we exaggerate their potential danger. Visions of utter chaos flit across our minds, replete with bodies colliding, injuries mounting, and out-of-control screaming filling the space. To suggest intentional movement in the early days of the school year, then, is cause for some teachers to question my sanity. For many educators, the priority at the start of the school year is establishing authority and order in the classroom, minimizing the potential for chaos, and holding students' attention (usually for laying the ground rules of the class). However, I maintain that all of these things are supported, rather than hindered, by incorporating structured movement into the class session right away.

This can be done in simple, basic movements such as getting students up from their chairs and asking them to walk over to a different area in the room where they will sit on the floor. The acts of standing from a seated position, walking (even just a few steps), and then sitting on the floor (which requires a deeper range of movement for legs and hips) all serve to activate different areas of the brain and contribute to increased attention. This movement needn't be chaotic. Students can move in small groups so that not everyone is walking about the space simultaneously. By introducing simple movements like these from the first day, students learn to listen to our directives and keep themselves respectful of the order we, their teachers, aim to uphold in the classroom. They get accustomed not just to movement itself, but also to *how* we'd like that movement to happen in our shared space.

Although movement contributes to increased attentiveness, it also serves to support a body's well-being. Keeping this in mind can encourage us to build in movement opportunities for our students whenever possible. Still, I understand the discomfort that some teachers feel about getting kids out of their seats in the first days of the school year. Things are already harried, and students may be anxious about all the newness of an unfamiliar teacher, classroom, and/or school. If movement isn't feasible, then, but keeping the students' attention after ten or fifteen minutes on the third day proves challenging, there is another way to regain their attention. That is to introduce novelty.

Of course, this early in the school year nearly everything is novel to the kids, but by the second week, if students have been sitting in the same seat each day, their attention may begin to wane. If that happens, then incorporating some element of alteration in the room can help. For example, we might employ an interesting and different communication style, such as speaking in a tone or accent we haven't used before as we explain something we need them to pay attention to. Or, we could stand in and draw their attention to a portion of the room we previously ignored. We might, instead, sit on the floor as we speak, inviting them to pay closer attention, perhaps even crane their necks or stand at their desks in order to see us.

Novel elements alert the brain to perk up and pay attention. If it isn't obvious, this is another invaluable tool in the teacher's tool kit. It's natural for the human mind to wander, to scan the environment for elements it deems noteworthy, and to drift from the immediate presence of external stimuli to the inward thread of thought, memory, or imagination. For this reason, we need a variety of methods that will effectively draw students' attention back to the content or task of the class lesson or activity.

My favorite way to introduce novelty is to manipulate the physical environment of the room. At first, in the early weeks, the changes can be minimal (such as having the kids sit in different seats each day), to support the students' acclimation to the overall space. Later, though, when the kids are absolutely comfortable in all areas of the room (usually at some point in October), I introduce bigger changes that really catch their attention. The next two chapters will cover those. For now, let's consider small ways to introduce novelty into the physical space in the early weeks of the school year.

Changing the physical environment a few times in the first few weeks helps students come to expect that change is a predictable structure in your classroom. It is wise to set the expectations for this early, so students are not jarred when changes occur later, but instead are intellectually awakened and supported by them.

The physical environment can be changed in subtle and obvious ways. Moving the furniture is one obvious way to manipulate the environment, but keeping the furniture as is and moving students to different seats is a more subtle way to shift their perspective on the environment for them (see Figure 4.1). In this way, the room itself is unaltered, so kids can become familiar with it, but their perspective changes daily, allowing them to see and feel the space slightly differently from one day to the next.

FIGURE 4.1
Though the furniture remains stationary for the first few weeks in my class, students will move frequently, so they have a chance to experience learning from each table and with each of their peers before assigned seats take hold.

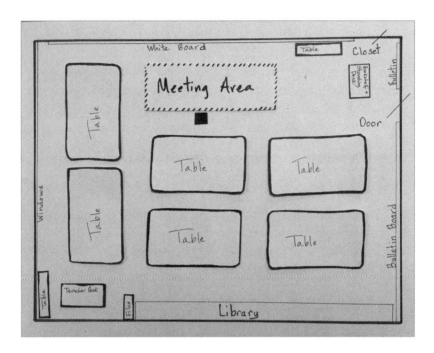

Following is a list of ways to create changes to the environment in the early weeks of school, without making drastic changes to the physical arrangement of the room. Whether you use one or more of these ideas will depend on your "read" of your students coupled with your own sensibilities. It may help to keep in mind that the goal is to keep your students aware without making them feel uneasy about too much change too soon and without letting them become too attached to a single spot in the room.

- Require that students find a new seat each day for the first week, and that they sit next to someone new each day. (If you want to assign seats, wait until the second week; that way you can observe how students interact with one another and make better-informed decisions about seat assignments.)

- Keep one or more areas of the room off limits for the first week or so. These might include the classroom library, conference table, or technology zone. Introduce those areas slowly, unveiling them one day but not letting students use them until the next day or only allowing small groups to explore them each day until everyone has had a chance to learn the purpose and behavioral expectations for those areas.

- Instead of assigning seats, assign partnerships and small groups to work together. Change those assignments each day (or every other day) throughout the second week until each student has had the opportunity to work with every other student in the class. By changing partners and groups, they'll necessarily change seats, too, but those seats will not be "assigned."

- Introduce new seating arrangements (by moving furniture) a few times in the second and third weeks. Once students have experienced the room from different vantage points (seats), they should begin to see the space in a variety of furniture arrangements. Thereafter, you can choose specific seating arrangements for different purposes that are determined by the goals of your lessons and units.

WHY THIS IS HELPFUL

I've found that introducing frequent alterations, like those listed previously, in the first weeks of school (being mindful to keep them subtle enough not to jar students as they acclimate to the new class experience) helps kids quickly embrace the dynamic and flexible nature of the classroom. This prepares them to approach change with an open mind and to appreciate how it prepares their brains to pay closer attention.

Later, when we want to make bigger changes that align with particular units or learning activities (see "New Units of Study"), our students understand that these changes are purposeful and supportive, rather than disruptive or distracting.

OTHER CONSIDERATIONS

Whereas adapting to the external environment is supported by the ideas discussed earlier, developing an inner concept of belonging requires a little more attention. Typically, students come in on day one and—whether they are assigned to a seat or choose one on their own—sit in their seat. Then, they tend to head directly for that same spot in the room every time they enter thereafter. In some instances, an adventurous type will try to claim a new seat, but the previous occupier cries foul and begs the teacher to restore the intruder to his or her rightful place. This creates a pattern, at first, and soon becomes a part of the student's identity as a member of the class. The physical station is no longer just a seat in the room, but becomes, in the student's mind, "where I belong" in the room, a safety zone. When we allow this to happen, the student identifies that small spot in the room as "my spot" and a primal sense of territorial ownership kicks in, creating bigger challenges down the line. Similarly, students can become attached to the idea that those sitting around their "spot" are the only students with whom they'll need to interact for discussions and collaborations. This creates an "us-and-them" mentality that does not support a rich and diverse learning community.

When the teacher needs to change seats later, for any reason, a disturbance is created in the minds of the students who are being asked to move. As far as their brains are concerned, the teacher may as well say, "And now I'm going to pose a threat to your safety." Thanks to Judy Willis's work (www.radteach.com), we know that this kind of brain signal is bad news for our students' experience. Registering as stress in the brain, this "threat" effectively shuts down the very part of the brain we need students to keep active during learning activities: the more evolved, higher-thinking brain. When the higher-thinking part of the brain shuts down, the primal reactive brain takes over and students default to survival mode. All of this presents as resistance from the student, and can even escalate into refusal to engage in the lesson of the day. Even compliant students who make the seat change and smile at the teacher to show all is well might have a difficult time focusing on the lesson for the rest of the period, because their brains are flooded with cortisol (known as the stress hormone) and they're strategizing about how to save themselves from the predicament. For obvious reasons, we'll want to set kids up for success by avoiding this kind of problem.

By acclimating students to change regularly and early on, we prepare them to expect change and easily flow with it. Just think of all the ways this will serve kids, not only in our classrooms, but throughout their lives. After all, isn't change the only true constant we can count on? Isn't our world increasingly innovative, dynamic, and globally oriented? Additionally, we eschew the false sense of security afforded by the "one-seat and few-peers" model of the stagnant classroom and instead foster a deeper sense of belonging for each of our students by developing healthy working relationships with their teacher(s) and all peers through engaging, collaborative learning experiences in every area of the classroom. In this way, students come to recognize the classroom and the people in it as theirs and they cultivate ownership over their experiences within that community and space.

TRANSPARENCY

As always, it helps to share with our students the ideas behind our directives. In the early weeks, when we instruct our students to find new seats and neighbors, we meet little resistance, because everything is still new. If we wait to introduce change, our students will have already established their expectations of the class and will find the changes disturbing, as described previously.

Sharing the ideas can be as simple as taking the last few moments of class on day one to explain ourselves. We could say something such as "Students, one thing you'll learn pretty quickly here is that this class relies on what neuroscience teaches us about how our brains work. Since everyone's goal is to successfully learn what this course has to teach, we are going to be using some methods to support our brains' work in that endeavor. Over the course of the year, you'll learn a lot about [course content], but you're also going to learn about how your own brain works, which will let you take control of your learning in other areas of your life. For now, I'm going to ask that every time you come into this room for our first week together, you choose a seat that is different from the one you chose previously, and that you sit near people you haven't yet sat near. Tomorrow, I'll explain how this simple little trick is going to help your brains get smarter."

The next day, display a reminder that students should choose new seats and neighbors. When they're in new seats, you can explain that the novelty of a new perspective on the room and the chance to meet and talk with new classmates (or reacquaint with peers they haven't seen or talked to in a couple of months) will help build the class community while keeping everyone's brains alert to what's happening in the still-new environment. It will help to say that neuroscience shows us that people have more positive learning experiences when they're immersed in a supportive community and that novelty in the environment (like the new perspective offered by a different seat near different peers) helps the brain to be more alert.

BUILDING COMMUNITY

New seats and neighbors are just the beginning, of course. We could ask students to take two minutes at the start of class to introduce themselves to their new neighbors and learn one thing about them, then get into the lesson of the day. However, if the bulk of the remaining class period has kids sitting still and silent in their seats, then the benefit of the changes implemented will be minimal

ACTIVE ENGAGEMENT

Consider how you approach staff meetings at school: Do you tend to always sit on a certain side of the table? Do you gravitate toward the same colleagues? Do you have a "comfort zone"?

Make a plan to gain a new perspective the next time you enter your meeting room. Choose to sit near someone you haven't sat next to recently; sit on the side of the room that is opposite the one where you normally sit.

If the next meeting is too far in the future, try doing this at home. Do you have a designated spot at the dinner table? Do you always sit in the same chair or spot on the sofa for relaxation time? Try taking a new space today. Notice how this affects your experience and awareness.

Write for two or three minutes on this experiment. (See Figure 4.2.) Be sure to include how and when you'll try this out with your students.

FIGURE 4.2

Two pages from my journal documenting a time I chose a different seat at a staff meeting

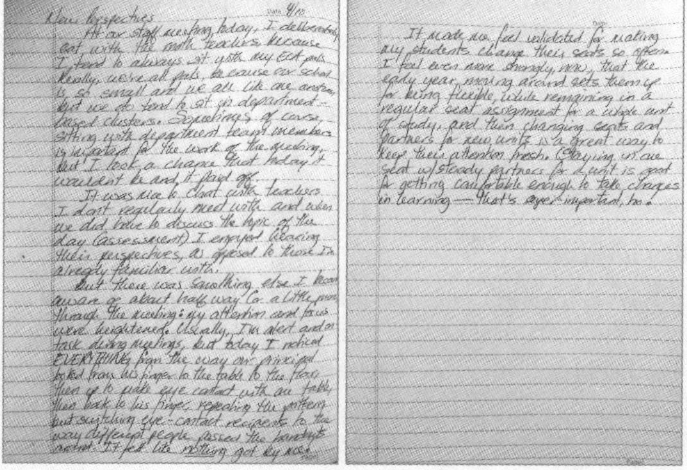

New Perspectives — Date 4/10

At our staff meeting today, I deliberately sat with the math teachers, because I tend to always sit with my ELA pals. Really, we're all pals, because our school is so small and we all like one another, but we do tend to sit in department-based clusters. Sometimes, of course, sitting with department team members is important for the work of the meeting, but I took a chance that today it wouldn't be and it paid off.

It was nice to chat with teachers I don't regularly meet with and when we did have to discuss the topic of the day (assessment) I enjoyed hearing their perspectives, as opposed to those I'm already familiar with.

But there was something else I became aware of about half way (a little more) through the meeting: my attention and focus were heightened. Usually, I'm alert and on task during meetings, but today I noticed EVERYTHING from the way our principal looked from his paper to the table to the floor then up to make eye contact with one table then back to his paper, repeating the pattern but switching eye-contact recipients to the way different people passed the handouts around. It felt like nothing got by me!

It made me feel validated for making my students change their seats so often. I feel even more strongly, now, that the early year, moving around gets them up for being flexible, while remaining in a regular seat assignment for a whole unit of study, and then changing seats and partners for new units is a great way to keep their attention fresh. Staying in one seat w/steady partners for a unit is good for getting comfortable enough to take chances in learning — that's super important, too!

or lost altogether. We also want to get our students out of their seats and engaging in meaningful talks with peers at intervals throughout the class.

For more details on orchestrating effective class sessions that deeply engage students, refer to Chapter 3 of this book.

NEW UNITS OF STUDY

After my students all left for the day, I pulled from the wall all the charts pertaining to our just-ended unit of study. That alone opened up the room by removing a lot of visual clutter. Next, I took down all the students' work from the past three weeks and freshened up our bulletin board with new paper in a brilliant blue hue, trimming the space with a crisp white scalloped border. Now I felt myself breathing more deeply and smiling more widely. Though I hadn't opened the windows, the room felt as if it had been swept through with a breeze of fresh spring air.

Now I walk through the space thinking about tomorrow's lesson. We'll be launching our unit of study on poetry. I will gather my students in our meeting area to read and briefly discuss Robert Frost's "The Road Not Taken" because I love the suggestion of individuality and choice it brings up, which aligns beautifully with the big idea I want students to glean from this unit of study (each person's experience matters), as well as the glimpse it provides into the paradox of choices (to make one is to deny another, thereby expanding and limiting experiences simultaneously). Though we'll start with Frost, students will read a rich diversity of poets and works, and write from their own experiences. Then I'll have the kids work their way around the room to engage in silent, written discussion of the same piece (see Figure 4.3). I've printed the poem on large poster paper along with open question prompts (I like to offer supports and prompts, but I don't require students to use them), so I will need a lot of room in the space. I decide I want four large tables, one for each poster, and that the students will just walk and stand around them to write their contributions (see Figure 4.4), so I push all the unnecessary tables to the periphery of the room. But what to do with all those chairs?

FIGURE 4.3
Students write responses to a poem (and to one another) in this silent read-and-respond activity. Working their way around the room, they contribute to different written conversations about the same poem on different charts of paper, and then end up where they'd started to read responses to their original comment.

FIGURE 4.4

The tables against the wall serve as a landing space for backpacks and other belongings.

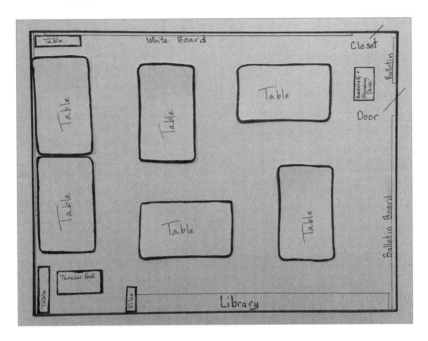

Thinking further about how the class session would flow, I realize that I hadn't accounted for a few key parts: the students' arrival, the initial walk-and-talk to access prior knowledge, and the culminating discussion. I envision the start of the period: Where will kids put their backpacks? They'll drop them on the tables along the back wall of the room. How will the walk-and-talk work? We'll walk a crisscrossing path around and between the four remaining tables and I'll lead the pack. The discussion . . . Ah! I'll place the chairs against the tables at the periphery and along the other three walls, facing into the center of the room so that when everyone sits for the last discussion, we'll be arranged in a big circle and facing one another.

After arranging all the furniture, I take one last look at my room. I feel a wave of satisfaction and a sense of eagerness for tomorrow's first class session. I'll put the last touches—the poem posters—in place in the morning, before the students arrive. Now I can go home and rest easy, knowing that our classroom space is ready for a productive launch into our poetic work.

The start of a new unit of study is an ideal time to freshen up your classroom space with a revised room arrangement. Most teachers I've worked with agree that the start of a new unit should "feel" different, not only for the students, but for us, too. We like when there's a change in the air, when there are new challenges and triumphs to experience. We want it to feel like the dawn of a new season, bright with hope and charged with positive anticipation. Walking into a physically altered environment sends a powerful signal to everyone's brain that there's reason to pay close attention, that there is something new to learn here.

Interestingly, we don't just receive a neurological cue to pay attention when there is novelty in the environment; we also experience increased executive function (intellectual processing), so this is a great time to introduce a new concept, such as one pertaining to our new unit of study. It could be tempting to spend that first session in the altered space letting students acclimate to it. However, teachers might find it more valuable to use that time to get kids actively engaged in the intellectual challenge of considering new course information.

Although it is important for students to get acquainted with new furniture arrangements (particularly since they'll need to safely navigate the room during brain breaks), that will happen organically in the process of moving through class sessions over the first few days of a new unit. Better to capitalize on the brain's readiness to dig into intellectual challenge right away, then.

The following are some questions that naturally arise when considering new room arrangements to reflect a shift in content study, as well as my answer to each of them:

- **How different should the room be?** Even subtle changes have a palpable effect on awareness, so the degree to which you alter your room should match your own comfort level and time, as well as the learning experience you have planned for your students. The minimalist will want to ensure that the change is noticeable immediately to students as they enter the space. Those of us who welcome a bit more drama can employ their creativity to their heart's desire, limited only by the parameters of the room, available furniture and accessories, and their administrators' degree of consent.

- **What if my classroom furniture doesn't move or the current arrangement is ideal for our work and for our community?** Visible change doesn't require furniture rearrangement. Consider adding plants, artwork, or special lighting, if these don't already exist. Other ideas include putting up fresh paper or borders to existing display boards in the room, dressing the windows, or putting down a throw rug and pillows in newly designated areas. Change can be audible, too. You could have instrumental background music playing as your students enter on the day a new unit is launching. Even placing something on each student's desk or table can be enough novelty to wake up their brains—perhaps colored place mats, playful doodle paper, or even a new set of pencils for each child would be enough "newness" to signal the brain to pay attention. Experiment within your means and boundaries and have fun with this.

- **Who has time for rearranging a classroom?** With all of our work planning, grading student work, and the myriad tasks in a typical day, redecorating can seem like just another task on a long list of to-dos. We want to make sure that when we set aside precious time for any activity, it is going to pay off in increased student focus and learning. This will! That said, it needn't require a big investment of time to be effective. My room arrangements often were complete inside of ten minutes, and the physical work was beneficial to me, because it got my body moving and my mind off the intellectually rigorous demands of planning, grading, research, and composing. If ten minutes feels like too much, enlist your students to help at the end of the day before a new unit begins and the job will be done in five minutes or fewer. Additional bonus: when students help, they can better understand why the change is helpful.

- **What if my administrators are opposed to changing classroom layout?** If this is the case at your school, it would help to share some of what you know about how novelty affects the brain, so your administrators can revisit their previous thinking. Since the goal of every school is to maximize student learning, it'll be important to include the scientific evidence that supports the practice of altering the physical space to increase executive function (see Chapter 2). Invite your administrators to observe two class sessions: one before and one after you implement an environmental change. Sometimes people have to see with their own eyes or experience something to deem the concept valid. If administrators remain opposed, try some of the more subtle suggestions included under "What if my classroom furniture doesn't move . . . ?."

- **Is it enough to change peer partnerships and seat assignments?** It can be. Having a new partner or group is certainly reason for the brain to wake up and pay attention, because students are faced with making a "new" working relationship and will usually be inclined to want to make a good "first" impression. This might be less novel if all students have already worked together at some point in the year, but that can be hard to predict. I would suggest that your plans include ensuring that each student moves to a new seat assignment, if possible, giving them a shift of visual perspective.

- **The content of the course is new. Isn't that enough?** Surprisingly, encountering new content within a stagnant physical environment does not have the same effect as when the environment itself is different. Because the room feels the same as yesterday, the "context" of the course— or learning environment—signals to the brain that there is nothing new here, so there's no need to "wake up" and pay attention. Unfortunately, this requires students to put in more effort than their brains want to so they can deeply engage with (and learn) the new content.

- **How can I get my room to do more than just signal change? How can I get it to support the work we will be doing?** I love this question, because I think it shows that we often strive to achieve more for our effort and that we aim for synergy and alignment in our work and in our classrooms. We can absolutely find ways for the room to reflect and support the work kids will be doing in it (see Figures 4.1, and 4.4–4.9). For example, if the unit of study will call for a lot of whole-class discussions, we'll want the furniture to either be set up for that right away or foster quick, easy transitions into a whole-class oval or circle for better face-to-face communication (see Figure 4.5). On the other hand, if the students will be getting into group work right away, we'll want the groupings to be easily accessible: chairs and desks can be prearranged to host study groups (see Figure 4.6), or students can have assigned clusters but choose their individual seats within those clusters. If independent study will be the norm, then creating the layout that best supports that work would be in order (see Figures 4.1 and 4.7). It's always a good idea to ensure that the room matches and supports the work kids will be doing in the space.

FIGURE 4.5

In this formation, the class can sit on the outside of the rectangle, using the table space for notes and other materials. This fosters extended whole-class discussions.

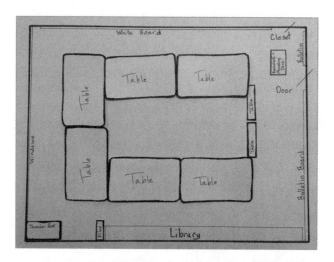

FIGURE 4.6

This setup can work for groups or stations, with or without chairs. Smaller groups might work better with the tables spread out, as in Figures 4.1 and 4.4.

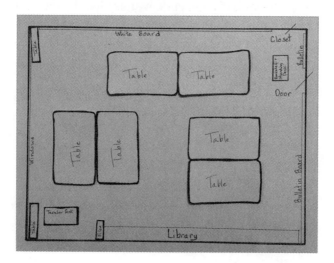

FIGURE 4.7

This setup allows for a change from the "basic setup" (depicted in Figure 4.1) without losing functionality. When students need some independent work space, I like for the tables to be spread apart like this. Students can still collaborate with others at the same table, of course, or move to a standing work station, or a floor seat, for more independence.

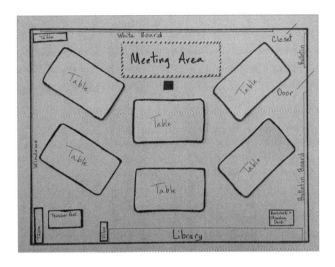

FIGURE 4.8

This arrangement makes for easy gallery walks to display and examine student work and other visuals. It can also be used for split-class discussions or debate prep.

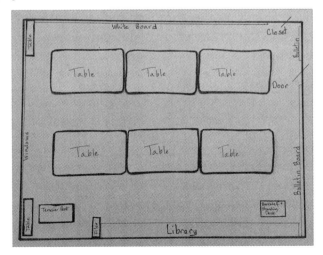

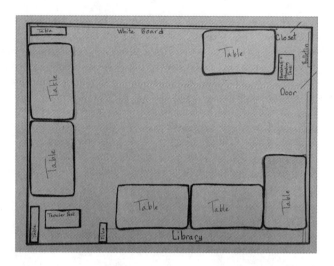

FIGURE 4.9

With the tables pushed out of the way, we can create a large oval of chairs for a more intimate whole-class "round-table" discussion, or use the open floor space for stage practice when reading plays; work space for large projects (such as poster making); expanding floor seating options for a flexible work space; increasing privacy or accountability by having students sit at tables facing walls and windows (great for digital assessments, because teachers can easily view screens).

ACTIVE ENGAGEMENT

Take three to five minutes to move your body. Take a brisk walk, dance to music, climb the stairs, or alternate jumping jacks and jogging in place. This, as you know, will prime your brain for some creative thinking.

Next, take out your yearly curriculum plan as well as your current unit and lesson plans. Start penciling in ideas for room arrangements that will support the work your students will be doing in the next weeks and months. You can take this one step further and create diagrams of these different arrangements, labeling them by unit, lesson, or week.

Then, reflect in your journal about the effects of moving your body before taking on a new challenge (aligning room design and curriculum!). Also write about planning your classroom layout as a component of your curriculum.

UNIQUE EXPERIENCES AND SPONTANEOUS FLEXIBILITY

In our study of Romeo and Juliet, I noticed that my students were having a hard time understanding some of the stage direction—namely, how the characters were situated in relation to one another. The best way to "get it," I decided, was to enact it. Our room was not ready for this, though, because we'd arranged the tables in a way that left no space in the room for a "stage" (see Figure 4.7).

"All right, I've got it," I said. "Everyone, put down your book and let's move the tables toward the back of the room." Instantly, the room erupted into chatter and movement. As the kids rearranged the room, I had them count off from one to six (the number of characters on stage in this particular scene), instructing them to remember their numbers. Once the tables were moved (see Figure 4.9), all the students gathered on the floor facing our newly created "stage" area and I chose a random set of characters (by number) to come up and demonstrate.

We carefully read through the scene as the "actors" modeled the action. Once the whole class had a visual sense of how the scene played out, I had the demonstrating actors integrate into new groups and all students worked, in groups of six, through the scene together, acting it out.

Within ten minutes, the scene acting was finished and the kids had put the room back together. We discussed the scene, this time from a place of clarity, as the students better understood the dynamics among the characters and were able to examine the implications of their actions.

When the entire classroom community is accustomed to operating within a fluid space, then moments of spontaneous flexibility are possible. Had my classroom been a place of immobility before the Shakespeare unit, and had students been conditioned to working from the same seat in the same place all year long, then they may have been so distracted by my instruction (to rearrange the room) and the sudden discomfort it would likely have brought on (just imagine: the "security" of their defined roles and places suddenly disrupted and all the students "exposed," out from behind their assigned desks, expected to perform a confusing play) that they'd have a hard time focusing on the content of the play. Such an incident would not yield deeper understanding of the play itself, but would instead become an exercise in how to behave outside of everyone's comfort zone within the classroom.

Had the students not been accustomed to a flexible classroom (and being seen and heard by all their peers), they wouldn't have been able to concentrate on Shakespeare's direction but instead would've been inundated with managing their sudden self-awareness and insecurity when I'd asked them to rearrange the room and act out the play. As it was, their learning process was supported, rather than disrupted, by this spontaneous change.

Many of the learning experiences we orchestrate for our students are planned. This is essential to a well-run, effective classroom. However, we also need to be responsive to our students' needs in any given moment (see Figure 4.10). Sometimes, plans don't work out the way we'd envisioned and students are left confused or with more questions than understanding. In such cases, we have to help them bridge the gap between where they are and where we need or want them to be. Sometimes, it's enough to pause a lesson and host an impromptu Q and A. Other times, our kids will need an opportunity to engage in meaningful movement to viscerally experience the concepts just outside their mental grasp, as my students did for this *Romeo and Juliet* scene. In these instances, the setup of the room can be an important factor in fostering learning-supportive movement.

The key to creating a high-functioning fluid space is to *think* fluidly about our classrooms. Often, we think of our classroom setup in static terms and try to make the kids and work fit into that static arrangement, rather than thinking about how we can change the room to suit our educational needs. Whether it's because we put a lot of thought into the room's original setup at the start of the school year (and don't want to invest more time or effort in it) or because we think the furniture can't function differently than it already functions, we tend to be resistant to seeing the room in new ways. The best way to break this habit is to engage in change routinely. When we push ourselves to try new arrangements, we make discoveries about ourselves and our students and are better able to see how the physical space can support or inhibit learning. Likewise, when we invite our students into the thought process, they can provide new perspectives about how to use the room.

FIGURE 4.10
This anchor chart helps students recall the genre structure we encounter in Romeo and Juliet. *Valuable as such visual references are, though, creating a fluid, flexible space can also be a vital support to the learning process.*

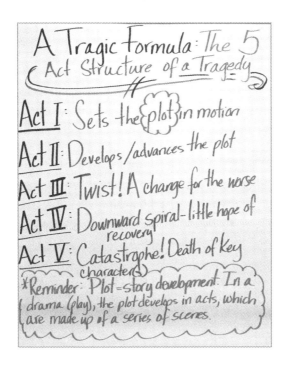

Dr. Carla Cappetti, one of my professors in college, often changed the desk arrangements before we students arrived to class. Sometimes, she'd have us rearrange the room during a class session. Although she did not explain why she did this, at first, it quickly became evident that she viewed the room and its furniture as objects in service of our learning. She had a dynamic and fluid perception of the space as a component of our studies. For example, when she was going to lecture (which was not often and never lasted for very long), the desks were arranged in rows facing the front of the room;

for small-group discussions, the desks were rearranged into clusters of three to six, positioned so that group members could face one another; for partner work, desks were arranged side by side in pairs; for whole-group talks, we made a large circle of our desks or chairs, pushing the extras off to the perimeter of the room. Not having experienced such a shifting classroom environment before, I remember feeling unnerved and noticing my classmates' awkwardness when these changes first started, but soon we all adapted and our class became one of the liveliest and most enriching of my college experience. In fact, I began to wonder why all teachers didn't use space like Dr. Cappetti did.

When we delve into the role of the physical space in the learning experiences we conduct for and with our students, we tend to realize that we don't need as much furniture in our classrooms as we once thought we did. Time and time again, I've worked with teachers who had too much furniture in their room, inhibiting movement and curbing their plans for small-group work or flexible arrangements, and who believed that they absolutely needed every piece. On deeper inspection, though, they were able to discover that they were holding on to furniture that was not earning its keep in the space.

For example, one teacher had a big table (similar to the size depicted in my classroom diagrams, Figures 4.1, 4.4–4.9) that she used to display books at the start of each unit of study. The books usually remained displayed on the table throughout the unit and students would borrow from the display. The table served no other purpose throughout the school year. I asked the teacher if there was another way to display books without using the bulky table. She looked around her room and said, "No. I need the table." I picked up the books from her table and walked them over to her whiteboard, which extended the entire width of the classroom, and propped the books on the marker tray along its base. There was plenty of space left over for her markers and erasers, and the books didn't interfere with any of the notes she'd written on her board that day (she tended to refrain from writing toward the bottom of the board). "What about this?" I asked. The teacher stood at the back of the room and took in the display.

"Can you see all of the books?"

She nodded and raised her eyebrows, suggesting her surprise.

I pointed to her classroom bulletin board—also a large display with a chalk/marker tray—and said, "If you have more books in a particular unit, you could also use that space to display them. What do you think?"

She smiled and said, "It works!"

We were able to reclaim a nice chunk of space in her classroom by removing the six-foot table that had once served a minimal, singular purpose. That gave her and her students more room to move around, spread out, and play with different furniture arrangements in the room. What's more, that teacher found the increased space so refreshing that she later removed three more pieces of furniture that she was finally able to see were not essential to her students' use of the room. Within weeks, she and her students were using the space more actively and fluidly. The result was profound. Teacher and students were more energized and inspired than they'd been when they stuffed themselves into a static, cluttered space that limited their movement.

Another teacher I worked with said he loved the idea of creating a meeting area for whole-class lessons but there was "no way" he could make it work in his small classroom. When we went into the space together, I observed his students' desks lined up in rows and generously spread out. In one corner of the room was a large teacher space with a big desk conjoined with a long, wide table, squaring off the corner of the room. Behind the desk were three file cabinets, a bookshelf, and another table (this one narrow, but also long) lined with piles of paper. In the front of the room were two more bookshelves and another large table holding student supplies. The back of the room was lined with closets that had closed doors on which the teacher had hung store-bought posters on grammar and punctuation, and one with quotes about reading.

Before addressing the myriad tables that served mysterious functions in the room, I asked about the students' desks. The teacher explained that the rows kept everyone facing the Smart-board, where the main teaching happened, and that all the space around each desk allowed the teacher to comfortably confer with his students individually.

"Have you ever tried clustering the desks into groupings of four or even six?"

The teacher took a deep breath while shaking his head. "I don't see how my kids will stay focused if they're facing each other like that."

I reminded my colleague that his goal was to create a meeting area, which would enhance attention during whole-class lessons. "This could also open up new possibilities for small-group work and group conferences," I said, "and the kids might surprise you with how well they can focus during independent time when facing one another. If not, you can always help them learn how to work effectively in this kind of seating arrangement." Of course, teaching kids how to work effectively in more collaborative and flexible seating patterns does take practice, time, and patience.

He agreed to give the clustering a try, and we moved the desks into groups of four. By now, we'd spent only about three minutes in his room and the transformation was eye-opening. Suddenly, there was more space than the teacher knew what to do with!

Perhaps more inspiring was the teacher's changed demeanor as he looked at his newly arranged room. Now he was gesturing with his hands as he walked through the space saying how he'd have the students gather here for the next day's lesson and how (he moved a chair to the front of the room, facing the newly created space, as he spoke to me) he'd sit facing the kids and explain to them how this new seating arrangement was going to enhance their learning experiences. I smiled as I listened and watched this now highly animated man talk out his new vision for class time, and marveled at *his* transformation from nervous and uncertain, stiff, tight, and quiet—just five minutes earlier—to confident, excited, smiling, spreading his arms and moving through the space as if he'd just realized he wasn't cramped inside a closet but was free to spread out and breathe new life into the space.

When we allow ourselves to imagine new possibilities and consider solutions to potential problems, rather than staying stuck in stagnant thinking (and room arrangements), we can create effective change in our classrooms with a minimal investment of time or effort.

ACTIVE ENGAGEMENT

Move your body for three to five minutes with an activity you enjoy, and then stretch gently while breathing deeply. Get your journal, pen, and a glass of water, and settle in for five to ten minutes.

Recall a time in recent days when your classroom activity could've benefited from rearranging the physical space. Did you have students working in groups without being able to properly face one another? Were your students particularly energized at any point—or the opposite—and might've had deeper engagement in the activity if they had been able to use the room differently? Was there an activity that didn't go as well as you'd hoped that might've benefited from taking just a few minutes to "set the stage" for that work by rearranging the furniture?

Write out your thoughts about this. If you could do that activity again, with the same students, how could you redesign the space for increased engagement?

Next, think about the lessons you have planned for the next few class sessions. Where might the students benefit from a quick furniture change? If you can't think of a place now, write out a scenario in which you ask your students to help rearrange the room to open up more space and then have everyone stand in a big circle so everyone can see everyone else while having a whole-class discussion for three to five minutes. Write out how your students will return the furniture to its place quickly and safely and continue with the work of the session.

CHAPTER 5

THE STAGES

CHALLENGING THE NOTION OF CONTROL

It's mid-November, and my sixth-grade students are working on their realistic fiction drafts. Our lesson ended about ten minutes ago, and I've just pulled a small group (Lamar, Suzie, and Ralph) to our meeting area for a quick conference on elaboration (see Figure 5.1). From my seat on the floor, I notice movement toward the back of the room and look up to see Jerry, paper and pen in hand, leaving his assigned seat and walking toward the windowsill, where he settles back into his work while standing.

FIGURE 5.1
This lesson chart shows a definition of the writing skill I'm teaching, as well as my teaching point and some examples of how to use the skill in writing.

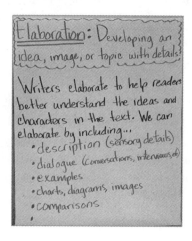

I begin my small-group lesson by reminding the young writers that to elaborate is to help the reader understand something by including a more detailed explanation of the concept. As I speak, I see that Karina is signing herself out of the room for a bathroom break. The lesson is going well, because my students remember learning about elaboration and trying it in class last week; they just haven't used elaboration effectively in their own stories yet. When I suggest they choose one underdeveloped piece of their stories and write it out on a separate piece of paper, adding details to elaborate, they all do so fairly quickly. I look away from them for a moment and notice Madison and Paul moving with their stories into the library alcove to chat about their work (and I appreciate that they are considerate of their tablemates' need for quiet and concentration).

When my small group has shown me their rewrites and demonstrated their ability to elaborate in their own stories, I send them back to their independent seats and take a moment to jot some notes for myself about their work before gathering another group of kids for small-group instruction on punctuating dialogue. As I write, someone walks past me, and I look up to see Daniel walking and stretching his arms high and wide. I smile, because it makes me happy to see that he's learned how to manage his energy and focus. He'd been working diligently on his writing for about fifteen minutes, and now he's taking a quick walk break. Sure enough, after circling the room three times, he settles back in at his table and continues working on his story.

I begin to make my way around the room, and as I walk by one table, I hear Shae whisper to Manny, "Will you help me for a second? I just want to know if this part makes sense." Again, I smile, because my students have learned how to lean on each other rather than depend solely on me to manage their needs and provide all the support. I'm also moved by their investment in the quality of their work—if they didn't care, they wouldn't be seeking feedback!

As a new teacher, I recognized my responsibility for students' safety, academic learning, and social development, but I'd confused that responsibility with control. I thought I had to *control* everything in the room to fulfill my duties. How wrong I was! Thankfully, I've since learned that being in "control" of everything diminishes my students' ability to learn and my ability to teach.

Just think how different the scenario described previously would be if I were the authority in charge of making every decision in the classroom. At the start of my lesson with Lamar, Suzie, and Ralph, either Jerry would've interrupted me to ask if he could work by the window or he'd have politely waited until I'd finished the lesson. If he'd waited, he would've spent five minutes or so distracted from his own work, just watching me until he could get my attention to ask permission. Instead, he felt the need to stand and took it upon himself to do so, losing only moments of focused work time in the process—the exact number of moments it took to gather his things, walk to the window, and resettle into the work. It couldn't have taken more than one minute.

The same is true for Karina and the others. But, because they were all empowered to decide what they needed and then to fulfill those needs without my involvement, they maximized *their* focus and productivity *and mine*. What's more, these kids will be able to manage their work time efficiently outside the realm of my classroom. They'll take these skills with them when they leave me.

It took me some time to get comfortable with kids being more autonomous in my classroom. I didn't just one day release all control and embrace lawlessness. Instead, I gradually released the constraints with careful planning and practice. I also talked with my colleagues about this process. I thought it was important for my students' other teachers to know we were moving toward more independence in my class (and why we were doing it), so those teachers could try it in their own classes, or at least so they would understand why their students might try (or ask) to do the same in their classrooms. For complete transparency, I'll share here that I encouraged my students to talk to their other teachers about how our methods improved our class flow, but I also explained that not all teachers would be comfortable with their students moving about the room at will. Preparing my students to be respectful of the conditions of different environments is important. I ask that they always respect those conditions and the variety of teacher styles they'll encounter throughout their schooling experience.

Recall that Jerry chose to continue his work while standing at the window. Three weeks before this particular class session, I'd introduced the concept of using a standing workstation to increase brainpower and mental focus. I demonstrated the practice frequently and guided all of my students through a trial session. I'd created three stand-up "stations" in our room and had the students cycle through so that each child had experienced it at least once. When the last students had experienced the stand-up station, I invited the students to use the stations any time they thought standing would help them focus.

The kids were not instantly cognizant of when their focus was fading. Noticing that, too, took practice. However, because we'd been using movement as a tool to wake up brain activity for a month or more at this point, the students were gaining awareness of their mental states and beginning to monitor themselves with increased independence. That said, there were times when I could see the signs of waning attention—a writer staring into space, a reader's eyes struggling to stay open—and suggest (or require) that the student take a walk break and use a stand-up station.

My coaxing paid off, as Jerry demonstrated. He had both embraced the power to attend to his own needs *and* trusted that I would not go back on my word and scold him for being out of his seat without permission.

Daniel had done the same. He did not interrupt my lesson to ask permission to take a walk break. He just got up and walked around the room, stretching as he went, and returned to his seat with renewed focus for his writing. I counted this as a triumph for that fall's work, because when Daniel arrived at my door that September, new to middle school, new to our building and community, he had been quite attentive to rules and had sought permission for everything. He wouldn't write a word in his own notebook without being assured that I condoned the writing. During the release-of-constraint phase for walk breaks in our early weeks of school that year, Daniel struggled to accept his autonomy. He'd asked

permission for every move he made, all of the time, despite my
repeated encouragement to consider his permission granted even
before he asked.

One day, I took a different approach. Rather than entertain
his question and, yet again, tell him he could move if he needed
to, I ignored Daniel's raised hand, thinking he'd finally "get" the
message if I stopped reinforcing his approval seeking. While teaching a small group on the carpet, I saw Daniel from the corner of my
eye but did not look directly at him. I continued with my lesson,
remaining attentive to the students in front of me. I hoped Daniel
would notice the other kids moving about the room without seeking
my approval (which they knew they'd already received when I
had—weeks earlier—invited them to do so). Instead, Daniel kept
his hand in the air until it tired, and then he switched to raise his
other hand. Still I ignored him (though it hurt me to do so), not over-
looking the fact that nearly five minutes had passed and Daniel was
not doing his work. A few minutes later, my small group returned
to their independent work seats and I motioned for Daniel to come
to the carpet.

"Daniel," I said, "I noticed that you've been sitting with your
hand in the air for the past eight minutes or so, waiting for me to
attend to you. What was it you've needed all this time?"

"I was wondering if it would be okay if I worked in the library,
because I'm a little distracted by the other kids at my table."

"That sounds like a great solution to being distracted. Why
didn't you just take your things and go to the library, then?"

"Well, because I should ask first."

"Why do you think you should ask first?"

". . . Because we're supposed to ask before we get out of
our seats?"

"That may be true in some places. Is that true in this classroom?"

"Um . . . no?"

"No, it isn't; you're right. Why do you think I want you to get
out of your seat when you need to in this class?"

"Maybe because that way we don't have to disturb you?"

CHAPTER 5: THE STAGES

"Well, it's true that sometimes I'm busy with other students when you need something and I like to give my complete attention to whomever I'm working with. Thank you for recognizing that. There's another reason, though. Do you think you can remember what I've been saying to your class these past weeks about getting out of your seat?"

"Yes."

"What have I been saying?"

"That if we need to move to a new spot or take a walk break, we should just do it?"

"Yes. Why do I want you to do that?"

"Well, I guess because then we can focus on our work better?"

"Yes, that's it. I want you to trust yourself. If you feel you need a walk break, a new spot to work in, or even a bathroom break, then I want you to take that break and get back to work rather than sitting and waiting for me to say you can do it."

Daniel nodded.

"I wonder if it might help for me to give you a permission slip that you can keep with you as a reminder that you may move if and when you need to. Would that help?"

Daniel smiled.

"Okay," I said, and I grabbed my pen and sticky-note pad and wrote this note:

Dear Daniel,

You have my permission to leave your seat any time you need to walk, use the bathroom, or choose a new workstation in order to better focus on your work.

Sincerely,
Mrs. Hernandez

I handed the note to Daniel. He read it and stuck it to the inside front cover of his writing notebook.

"One more thing," I said. "If I ever scold you for being out of your seat during independent work time, you can show me that note to remind me that I wrote it. Is that a deal?"

"Okay," Daniel said.

I offered my hand. Daniel took it with a smile, and we shook on it.

That little conference worked. I actually saw Daniel flip to the note in his notebook before getting out of his seat once or twice. He needed the reassurance of my permission. Eventually, he didn't need the note anymore. He'd embraced his freedom.

All of the students eventually embraced their freedom, though—as with anything else—some took longer than others. What's also important to note is that I had to acclimate, too. I'd intended for the kids to self-monitor *and* address their needs, but when they actually started doing it, I found myself fighting the urge to ask, "Why are you out of your seat?" There were also, early on, some opportunists who used their newfound freedom to avoid work, and perhaps there were even some who overused the privilege simply to test my sincerity and trustworthiness, but I see this as their right. After all, I had to earn their trust just as they had to earn mine. Soon, though, these little tests wore off and productivity increased.

TOUGH SPOTS

One area of teacher control that can be particularly challenging to shift our mind-set about is bathroom breaks. For me, this was a tough one. Letting students leave the classroom means allowing them out of our realm of supervision, and that can make even the most lenient of teachers nervous. What's more, schools tend to have set rules about this, so we have to make it work within the confines of schoolwide agreements. In my school, the system was simple: teachers should keep a record of who leaves the classroom when, should strive for no more than one student out of the classroom at a time, and should be able to account for each student's whereabouts at any given moment.

For me, being the keeper of "who's out and who's up next for a bathroom break" was taking up too much mental energy—energy I'd prefer to devote to teaching. I tried having kids write their name on a list on the whiteboard, where I could see it at a glance, but then I'd forget to monitor when the first child returned and the next could go, because I was caught up in my lessons and conferences.

I decided to call a class meeting and let the kids help me solve the bathroom problem. Together, we devised a system that both honored our schoolwide protocol and allowed students to take some ownership of the procedure. We created a sign-out/sign-in sheet (see Figure 5.2) to be left on a small table right by the door. When someone needed a bathroom or water break, they'd go to the sheet, sign themselves out (name, date, time), and go. Upon returning they had to sign back in by crossing off their entry. We added some rules to the sign-out system to avoid breaking school code:

- If someone else was out, the next person in line would write their name and date but save the time entry for when they actually left the room. (That way, there was a record of who was next in line.)

- If someone else was out, but the newcomer had an emergency and couldn't wait, they'd sign out with a capital *E* next to their name to indicate the emergency status, and they'd go. (At first, I monitored this closely, until all my students understood that this was not be abused or overused.)

- Anyone who awaited another's return would go back to their seat and monitor for the other's return *while continuing their classwork.*

FIGURE 5.2

This simple record-keeping sheet, that students complete independently, has relieved me of excess mental energy previously devoted to monitoring bathroom breaks, and allows me to focus more attention on the teaching and learning matters of my classroom.

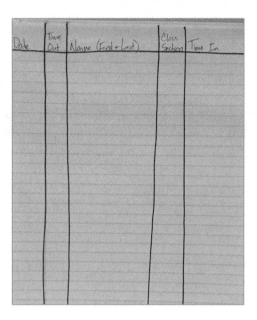

Once all students have acclimated to the system, it completely removes me from the equation, freeing up my focus for the more meaningful work of our class. It also encompasses an accountability record that could be checked in the face of any problems (though we've never had any). Because of this system, Karina was able to let herself out of our classroom without interrupting my small-group conference.

Another sticky area for teachers is student talk during work time. We want to make sure talk is focused on the work and is brief, lest it trickle into nonwork territory. I remember learning, as a young teacher, about "accountable talk" and thinking that I should be within earshot of, if not directly monitoring or participating in, all student talk for it to be "accountable." Thankfully, John Mayher's work showed me that "accountable" can include "exploratory" talk, which is necessary for kids to find their way around a topic or task. Once students demonstrate their ability to use exploratory/accountable talk without my participation, they should be empowered to do so as needed to support their learning and productivity (1990, 241). When I was ready, I devised a method that put my mind at ease and gave the students the freedom they needed to have productive talk during their work time.

Using a variety of methods throughout the school year, I teach students how to engage in productive talk as well as provide opportunities to practice it in the whole-class meeting area and small-group conferences, where I can eavesdrop or support as needed. Many of the lessons I use for this originated from my "forever partners" at the Teachers College Reading and Writing Project.

ONE SUCH LESSON GOES SOMETHING LIKE THIS:
Whole class gathered in meeting area for mini-lesson.

OPENING: I remind students that we have begun to revise our first drafts of a fictional story and say, "Often, when we read our first drafts, we notice problematic areas. Have any of you noticed a part in your story that just isn't working the way you'd hoped or intended it to work?" (Some students nod.) Next, I ask students to skim through their draft and locate one part that needs revision. "You can mark that spot, if you wish, or just remember exactly where it is. We'll come back to it in a few moments."

TEACHING POINT: Writers ask specific questions when they need help with their writing, by identifying and naming one problem they want solved.

DEMONSTRATION: I ask one student, Jason, to stand with me in front of the class. Holding my written draft, I point to one paragraph and say to Jason, "In this part, I'm trying to show that my character is feeling angry without just writing, *She's angry.* Will you read it and tell me if she seems angry?"

Jason accepts the request and begins reading the paragraph. As he does so, I address the other students.

"While he reads, will you quietly turn to your partner and talk about what made my question *specific*?"

I listen in while the students talk. Some repeat a portion of the teaching point, which is written on chart paper at the front of the room ("she identified and named the problem"), and others say things like, "She said exactly what she was trying to do in her writing, and that let the reader know what to look for."

I share with the class what I heard them saying, then say, "Let's find out what Jason has decided about whether my character, Ellen, seems angry."

Jason says, "Well, Ellen definitely seems annoyed, because right here [he points], you wrote, *While staring into the forest through her bedroom window, Ellen realized that her teeth were clenched together.* I think that if you want her to seem angry, you might want to revise this, because her emotion here just doesn't seem that intense."

"Ah," I say, turning to the class. "So I still have some work to do here, and thanks to Jason, I know that I need to make the action more intense to match the intensity of the emotion."

I turn back to Jason and thank him for his helpful feedback. He returns to his seat on the floor.

"Okay, everyone, now it's your turn."

ACTIVE ENGAGEMENT: "Recall that I asked you to find one place in your draft that is problematic. Take a moment now to construct a *specific* question—one that names the problem—and write that question on your draft paper." (I circulate as students busy themselves identifying and naming the problem, then writing it on their papers. I take a moment to coach as needed for students who "don't know" what the problem is, exactly. When most of the class has a question written, I stop them.)

"Put your thumb up if either yours or your partner's paper has a question written on it." I see that each partnership has at least one question between them, so I say, "That's fantastic! Go ahead and try the question out on your partner. Partners who are listening to the request, please say back to the sharing partner what makes the question specific and actionable." (Note: I might explain what actionable means, if needed. In this case, I didn't need to.)

The students ask their questions and partners respond. I stop them when everyone's had a chance to share, being careful not to let too much time pass. (Note: In whole-class lessons, my goal is for students to try the strategy I've just taught—to get a taste for it—but not to spend so much time on that trial that our lesson stretches into their independent and shared work time. When we all leave the meeting area, students will spend the remaining class time digging more deeply into the work. In this session, that work will include not just asking a specific question for feedback, but also allowing the partners to provide that feedback, and then writers will make any necessary revisions in their writing.)

CLOSING: "Students, today you learned that when you ask each other for help throughout the writing process, you can first identify and name a problem you want to address in your writing and then ask for *specific* feedback, just like I did with my partner, Jason, and like you practiced with your partner here in the meeting area. To practice this, I'd like you to start writing notes in your margin as you read your drafts. You can write things like, *Seems too vague* or *This part is confusing* or *Show emotion*. Then, when you ask a partner for feedback, you can be specific about what you're looking for."

In a lesson like this, I circulate while students work to notice what they're writing in the margins of their drafts. It takes some practice to get specific, so if the comments seem vague at first, I compliment the effort and coach students toward greater clarity by questioning their goals in that part of the writing. I might ask, "So what are you trying to convey in this part of your story?" or "What do you hope your reader will see or feel in this part?"

When I see that the majority of the class has done this work, I'll pause the writing workshop so students can try asking a partner for feedback using a very specific question. I listen in to as many partnerships as I can, and decide on subsequent lessons and conferences based on what I'm hearing. For example, student discussions may reveal common misunderstandings I can address with the whole group, or I might discover that a couple of kids are struggling with a certain skill or even that one student hasn't yet assimilated what I've taught in a previous lesson. Depending on what I learn as I listen in, I might decide to pull a student or small group for an impromptu conference, or I might make a note to plan a whole-class lesson for the next day.

As the year progresses and students get more and more practice talking and listening to each other *about their work*, I become freer to conduct my conferences and small-group lessons during the work sessions without fear that the other kids are off-task when talking. Which is why, when I saw Madison and Paul go into our library alcove to chat, I wasn't concerned or burdened with the distraction of wondering if I should interrupt my small-group lesson to go check in and ensure they were engaged in "accountable" talk. Because they'd learned how to lean on each other as collaborators and peer editors, I trusted that they were doing the work I'd asked and taught them to do. It might be worth noting that their conference was brief, because when I looked up again, as my small-group students were heading back to their independent work spaces, Madison and Paul were back at their seats working independently.

Though Shae and Manny didn't leave their table, they kept their voices low in consideration of their peers' concentration when they had an impromptu conference.

I want my students to know how to seek the help they need, but I don't want them to think I am the only person who can help them. This means they need to learn how to read their own work and others' critically *and* how to offer constructive feedback to peers. When they begin with peer support, they and I can get further along in our work than if the students came to me for everything. Of course there are some challenges that peers cannot help with, but to make our learning community most effective, my students and I make known our strengths and affinities. This way, if a writer needs help with removing excess in her writing, she knows she can ask our most efficient writer for guidance. If another writer wants more believable dialogue, he can ask the classmate who's strong in this area. If a writer needs support with punctuation in complex sentences, she can turn to our strongest sentence composer for help. For most peer conferences, though, their regular partners suffice. The nice thing about having regular partners is that kids get to know one peer well enough to build a strong working relationship.

After the first couple of weeks of the year (when I want kids to change partnerships daily to experience working with every other classmate), partnerships in my class last for an entire unit of study (six to eight weeks), and then they switch. Throughout the year, my students are partnered in a variety of ways, but I tend to employ a kind of gradual release method here (as I do with many other things in my teaching). My driving goal in changing partnerships is fostering thoughtful, deliberate decision making, meaning that I want the kids to figure out what good working partnerships feel like and how they operate, and to be able to experience working with every other student in the class to ascertain which peers make good working partners for them and which do not. That way, they can make informed decisions when choosing partners later on. Middle school students will almost always choose their friends as work partners at first, but with practice and reflection, they can learn to choose partners with whom they can focus and be productive, close friends or not. I always ask my students to reflect on their partnerships, whether I paired them or they chose them, and to determine what made the pairing successful or challenging.

Here is a general breakdown of the stages I tend to go through in the course of a year regarding partnerships:

1. Students choose seats; partnerships form by default.

2. I assign partnerships; students choose seats next to their partners.

3. I assign seats and partnerships.

4. Students reflect on which partnerships and seats have worked well for them so far and why; I listen and offer input.

5. Students choose partners, and I designate seats. (I aim to disperse energy fairly—not having all the dominant voices at one table or area of the room, for example.)

6. Students reflect on partnerships; I listen.

7. Students choose partners and seats.

8. Students reflect on partnerships and alert me to any issues or epiphanies.

Releasing control in the areas of movement, energy and focus management, bathroom breaks, and partnerships has had a significant beneficial effect on my students' and my efficiency and effectiveness in the classroom. The bigger benefit, though, is the increase in my students' self-awareness and advocacy. They've learned to tune in to their own learning styles, assess their own progress and challenges, and determine their own solutions. When they cannot clearly identify their challenge, they can turn to a peer or to me for support. Overall, though, my releasing control has resulted in a more empowered and reflective student body.

"CONTROLLING" STUDENT BEHAVIOR

This more empowered and reflective student behavior is evident in personal and emotional issues as well as academic ones. Take, for example, my student Kevin. Tall for his age, dark haired with a piercing gaze, Kevin is an imposing figure with a quick temper and a reputation for trouble. He's also funny and well liked by many of his peers. I got to know Kevin a little one year before he became my student, when I served on a lunch-detention rotation with other teachers. I would sit with my lunch and my work while the kids sat with theirs. Kevin attended lunch detention frequently.

I also learned about Kevin from his previous teachers. Occasionally, they'd tell about problems with him in the classroom: he refused to do the work, he argued with and sometimes physically confronted other students, he showed disrespect to his peers and teachers.

The year I taught Kevin was an interesting one. He wasn't the only eighth grader with that kind of reputation. There were enough of them to make the administrators offer us eighth-grade teachers a refresher course in protocol for classroom disturbances just before the school year started.

Being a language arts teacher affords a great deal of opportunity to tailor content to meet student needs, so I began that year with literature and lessons about personal growth, goal setting, and envisioning who each of us wants to be. This allowed my students to embrace the new year as an opportunity to break the threads of past years' narratives and start showing us, through their actions and words, who they wanted us to see when they walked into a room or down the hallways.

In addition to tailoring the curriculum, I vowed to do my part in helping change the negative patterns kids like Kevin (and his peers) had experienced. For Kevin, the problems usually stemmed from his anger at perceived wrongs and were almost always between him and a peer. He'd act out with harsh words or even a hit, shove, or kick. Then he'd be sent from the classroom to the principal's office, he'd serve detention, his mother would be called in for a conference, and he'd reluctantly write letters of apology and make false promises to avoid similar behaviors in the future. But the cycle repeated again and again. To me, Kevin appeared to be angry and frustrated. As far as anyone could tell, he wasn't learning how to interact positively with others, nor was he learning how to handle his anger productively.

When he had his first blowup in my classroom, it was during a reading workshop. I was conferring with one pair of students while the rest of the class discussed, in pairs, some prompts encouraging close reading of our shared text, *The Great Fire* by Jim Murphy. We were doing a lesson on making logical inferences and finding themes in informational texts (Robb 2013). Kevin and his partner, Suzanne, took a third member for this discussion, because Addison's partner was absent that day. I don't know what started the argument, but I heard a loud bang when Kevin slapped his hand on his table and yelled, "Shut UP, Addison!"

I walked quickly toward their table to find out what was going on. The rest of the room fell into near-silence as the other students turned to watch, too. Noticing the attention, Kevin flipped his hood up over his head and slumped in his seat. I thought, *Break the pattern, Katherine, break the pattern,* then asked, "What's going on, boys, and how can I help?" Addison looked at me and shrugged, turning his palms upward as if to say he had no idea what had caused Kevin's outburst. Kevin had been peeking from beneath the tip of his hood and, seeing Addison's gesture, blurted out, "Oh, right, Addison, so it's *my* fault. Come ON!"

"I'd like to hear your side, Kevin. What happened?" I asked, mindful of keeping my voice calm. Rather than answer me, though, Kevin kicked backward in his chair and shook his head while folding his arms across his chest. I turned to Suzanne and asked, "Can you explain what's going on?"

Suzanne said, "I think, well, Kevin said he thought the author was trying to show that the people shouldn't have built in Chicago, but then Addison said that that was obvious and we needed to explain *why* building there was a mistake. . . ." Her voice trailed off.

"It sounds like the boys disagreed about where the focus of the discussion should be, is that it?" Suzanne nodded.

"No!" Kevin said. "It wasn't that. It was that Addison wouldn't let me finish because he's a know-it-all who won't listen to other people's ideas!"

Now Addison was piqued. "That is NOT true! You called me an idiot so I said, 'Look who's talking,' and that's what got you mad."

Now Kevin put his head in his hands, elbows resting on knees, like he was bracing himself for what was coming next.

"Hmm," I said. "So you butted heads and derailed into personal insults, is that it?" Addison nodded, but Kevin was unresponsive. "It's a simple fix, then. Agree to avoid insults going forward, stay focused on the work, and move on."

Kevin looked at me with a grimace. "I'm not working with him," he announced.

"I'm not changing your partnerships at this point—the task is almost over. What you two just experienced is a simple bump that comes up when working with a new partner. You'll get better at working together *if* you move on, but if you quit, you'll fail to learn how to work together—and remember, Kevin, I expect you to learn how to work successfully with everyone in this room. You, too, Addison. Do you hear me?"

Addison nodded, but Kevin was still working down into his negative pattern, expecting the worst. "No way. I'm done. I'm not doing this with him." He kicked at the desk.

I could see that we were all headed into a trap that would consume the rest of our class time if we let it, so I looked at the clock, and then turned to the other students and said, "You have three minutes to finish finding evidence for your inferences and themes, and then you'll be sharing your findings with the whole class. Please get back to work."

Next, I addressed Addison and Suzanne. "You'll need to get this work done with or without Kevin, so I suggest you resume your discussion."

And finally, Kevin. "You seem upset. If you choose to take a break from the work, I'll understand. It's hard to focus when you're angry. But I'd prefer that you take your break outside the classroom, so others can focus. You are welcome to spend a few minutes across the hall [the principal's office] and then come back when you're feeling more cooperative." I walked the few steps it took to get to the door and opened it. As I stood there, I watched Kevin as he pondered the situation. He was being given a choice, not a command.

"Fine—I'm outta here," he said as he shoved the table leg with his foot, causing Addison's writing to falter.

Addison threw his arms up and opened his mouth in mock horror while looking to me as if to ask, "Did you see that?! What are you going to do about it?!"

In response, I simply closed my eyes briefly, nodded, and smiled. Addison seemed to understand: *calm down, be patient.*

Kevin made a show of leaving the room, huffing and stomping, shoving his chair under the table with a bang. Feeling it my duty to defuse the energy as much as possible for the benefit of the whole group, though, I stood calm and quiet. When he passed the threshold of our classroom into the hallway, I said, "Thank you, Kevin."

Not wanting the principal to receive Kevin under the usual conditions, I darted across the hall to introduce Kevin. The principal looked up from his computer as I said, "I offered Kevin a chance to take a break from our work for a few minutes. Can he sit in here for that?" The principal nodded and went back to typing. Then I turned my attention back to Kevin, who was making his way to an all-too-familiar seat and said, "Kevin, when you're feeling ready, please come back and join us. My plans for today's writing workshop might be interesting to you, and I don't want you to miss it. See you soon?"

Kevin looked at me briefly with raised eyebrows, and then turned away.

I thanked the principal and went back to my classroom. Once there, I asked Suzanne and Addison to please fill Kevin in on what he'd missed when he returned, and that was that.

One might wonder why I didn't address the name-calling or mediate a conversation between Kevin and Addison. The answer is that in my observation, Kevin wasn't ready for that. Once his anger was triggered, it was very difficult to defuse. My goal was first to help Kevin discover more positive coping mechanisms, such as the time-out I offered in this case, and to break the pattern of trigger, outburst, discipline/punishment. Later, we could work on interpersonal relationship building.

So how does this scenario fit into a chapter about releasing control? If I'd aimed for maintaining "control" in my classroom with Kevin and Addison that day, I'd have addressed the rules of conduct—no name-calling, no slamming hands on tables or kicking chairs, no yelling—rather than aiming to understand the problem and support a resolution. By asking the questions I asked, I modeled for the students that when a problem arises, we need to understand it to solve it. This takes a lot of practice, so I want my students to see, hear, and experience it often. I then want to encourage them to do the same in their own relationships, so they can better relate and work together.

Further, I practiced "close reading" of my students (Cunning-ham 2015). Kevin's body language, tone, and actions all indicated a level of anger that did not match the minor incident that caused it to flare up. Therefore, if I had continued to focus on the incident itself, I might have further inflamed Kevin's attitude, making him feel more defensive. Rather than minimize his hurt or fuel his fire, I chose to shift the focus from the "problem" to his choice. This gave him some power that would, I hoped, diminish the negative feeling of having been called out for a lack of intelligence. It worked, if not perfectly. By empowering him to make a choice, I broke the pattern of authority to which he'd become accustomed. I could have said, "Your behavior is unacceptable, and if you do not change it, you will have to leave my classroom," but that would only have affirmed my authority and his deviancy, which is exactly what I believe he was expecting. It would also have put me in the position of perpet-uating the very negative cycle I'd hoped to disrupt (see Figure 5.3).

It took a lot of effort to help Kevin break his negative patterns and reputation that year, but gradually he warmed to learning and practicing new ways of interacting with his peers. He became a little more trusting—not only of others, but also of himself. Before that year, Kevin was not trusted to make socially acceptable choices and, I believe, he was one of his greatest opponents. Yet he appeared to *want* to learn how to interact more positively with people.

It wasn't only Kevin who had some things to learn. His peers had some patterns of their own around him that needed restructur-ing, as did the adults at school, but when Kevin started to better manage himself, everyone else adjusted, too. A lot of this played out in our literacy classroom, where we practiced effective commu-nication methods and honed skills of respectful argumentation. In these lessons and activities, Kevin and his peers learned to commu-nicate their ideas, needs, and questions confidently and effectively. Of course, helping them experience real growth in this area meant that I had to let go of any lingering notion of "controlling" their actions and utterances in my classroom to encourage and accept their efforts to communicate, not just during planned discussions, but at any moment.

FIGURE 5.3

A paradigm shift for classroom management methods

PARADIGM SHIFTS IN CLASSROOM MANAGEMENT

Decrease ...	Increase ...
1. Adhering to strict rules Having clear conduct guidelines is helpful, but strict rules and a zero-tolerance attitude impede students' ability to develop coping mechanisms, ownership over the climate of the class, and strategies for solving problems that arise.	**1. Encouraging students to honor co-designed guidelines for behavior and conduct** When students contribute to the design and adoption of classroom conduct guidelines, they are far more inclined to honor them.
2. Doling out punishments This perpetuates an authoritarian model that infantilizes students, rather than providing them the space to develop important conflict resolution skills.	**2. Mediating conflict resolution discussions** When we serve as mediators, students get the much-needed practice of facing their opponents and speaking truthfully about their own experiences, as well as the essential practice of listening to others.
3. Isolating "problem students" Unless a student presents a real threat to others' safety, removing them from peers' proximity robs them and their peers of the chance to resolve upsets.	**3. Providing safe space for "cooling down"** If students are too upset to talk right away, offer a cool down period. During this time, the rest of the class can get back to work while those involved take a few minutes to write out, draw, or otherwise gather their thoughts. At the agreed-upon time, the conflict resolution discussion can occur in the classroom. While other students may not need to be directly involved in the talk, the chance to overhear it will benefit them, too.
4. Demanding apologies Young children need to be told to apologize, so they learn how and why they use this key social construct. However, upper elementary and secondary students should not be forced to apologize if the apology doesn't reflect their true feeling or perception. A forced apology is an empty one and only serves as a metaphorical Band-Aid that satisfies adults... they don't address the underlying wound.	**4A. Including peers in resolution process** When disruptions occur, all students need to learn how to deal with them effectively. Also, we want the group to be a trusting community, and that is fostered through honest appraisal of the triumphs and challenges within the group. They'll all take ownership and build stronger citizenship skills through shared responsibility.

	4B. Allowing for unresolved feelings and issues Rather than force a student to apologize, allow the students to honestly share their perceptions and feelings about the event. If an apology authentically arises, that will be great. However, in some cases it may be more appropriate for students to promise they'll try better next time, or simply to acknowledge that they disagree with one another and, having heard each other out, agree to move on for now.
5. Sending student(s) to disciplinarians outside the classroom While threatening behaviors need to be immediately removed from the classroom, minor disruptions and conflicts do not. Outside discipline measures deny students the opportunity to learn how to resolve conflicts in the moment.	**5. Handling nonthreatening upsets in the classroom, in the moment** Students need practice taking and demonstrating responsibility for their actions, inactions, and words. Taking time out of the academic focus to address upsets as a mediator, coaching students to listen to one another and respond respectfully, is time well spent. Students not only develop conflict resolution strategies in the process, but they also build empathy for others this way.
6. Perpetuating negative patterns "The definition of insanity is doing the same thing over and over again and expecting different results"—Albert Einstein. If a student or group of students is stuck in a negative cycle, we only perpetuate that negativity by responding to their upsets in predictable ways and following the established disciplinary routine.	**6. Disrupting negative cycles** In subtle ways, we can help students break negative patterns by offering a different response than they expect from us when conflict occurs. They will only learn new behaviors when we model new behaviors and provide opportunities for them to practice new behaviors.

That year, Kevin learned how to talk about what bothered him, rather than simply react in angry outbursts. He learned that *he* influenced his own experiences and wasn't just a victim of others' discontent with (or distrust of) him. He came to recognize that he was perpetuating the negative cycle with his own words and actions, and he worked to turn that around. Gradually, he devised alternative methods to the problems that came his way, and it was imperative that I give him the room to try these new methods.

Not ready, at first, to face his upsets directly and without anger, he learned instead to get up from his seat and find a new place in the room to calm down. Occasionally, he'd come to me and say,

"I just need to get out of here right now," and I'd let him leave the room for a longer, more private walk break. (Sometimes I'd give him an errand, such as delivering papers to the office two floors below our classroom, just to provide an excuse for his being in the hallway.) Other times, especially during reading, he would crawl under a desk in the back of the room to focus on his book. He even learned to ask me for help with his work when it was too challenging, whereas before, he would simply shut down and refuse to do the "stupid assignment."

Kevin helped me learn that it wasn't enough for me to be an effective "close reader" of students; I had to help them learn to closely read themselves. That was the only way they would be able to self-assess, manage, and advocate for themselves, but empower-

---

ACTIVE ENGAGEMENT

Take a few moments to raise your heart and respiratory rates through movement. Try doing elbow-to-opposite-knee hops (or simply bring your right knee up to meet your left elbow, then switch, without hopping) and a few jumping jacks. It doesn't take much to get the blood flowing! To extend the exercise, jog in place or simply keep switching from the knee-elbow movement to the jumping jacks and back for up to five minutes.

Next, grab your journal and begin to either list or write about all the ways you "control" the activity in your classroom. Reflect, in writing, on how these responsibilities keep you from attending to the deeper learning experiences you want to guide your students through.

Choose one area of "control" and brainstorm a couple of ideas for shifting the responsibility to your students so they can be empowered to manage it. Plan to present your idea to your students the next time you are in class together. For maximum "buy-in," explain the problem and your goal and ask your students to brainstorm some possible systems. If you implement an idea that comes, at least in part, from them, they'll embrace the change more fully than if you simply state your own new "rule."

---

ing them to do that required me to shift my idea of what classroom management should look and feel like.

BEGINNER BUMPS AND TRIUMPHS

MOVEMENT

It's our second week of using movement in the classroom, and I'm feeling encouraged. The first week went well, but the kids were only doing standing stretches, jumping jacks, and running in place behind their chairs. Today, I think we're ready to try walking around the classroom.

The eighth-grade students and I have already done a quick writing exercise (a three-minute freewrite) in response to a brief audio clip from NPR about a wrongly accused young man who was incarcerated without trial and whose father fought hard for five years to free him (WNYC 2013). Everyone is settled into the class and has already begun thinking about our topic of the day. We are in a unit I call Building the Habits of Success, which focuses on polishing and building on existing literacy skills through short texts and writing assignments on topics that are provocative and deeply meaningful in the students' lives. After a brief sharing of our ideas, I say, "Before we get into today's lesson and really grapple deeply with this idea of 'guilty until proven innocent,' let's get our bodies moving." I notice that the kids don't protest as they did on previous days. They actually seem to perk up at the suggestion, and I mentally note the progress.

"Instead of just moving at our seats," I continue, "let's give ourselves a chance to really spread out. Today, I'd like for us to walk together around the room. We're all going to need to be very careful not to bump into each other or trip over any obstacles in the way, okay?"

The kids appear to agree, so I say, "I'll put on a song and we can walk until it's over."

At that, everyone gets up and starts walking willy-nilly in random paths around the room while I head for the iPhone dock. (Note: I chose Annie Lennox's "Little Bird," in part for the beat, which is perfect for walking, and also because it wasn't likely to be a song the kids would know well. For our first trial with music, I didn't want the kids to be overly excited by hearing a song that they felt strongly about.) When my song is playing, I turn around and see that kids are everywhere, someone's jumping over a chair, someone's kicking a backpack out of their way, and I realize that this won't work. We need structure. I stop the song and put my hand in the air. Recognizing my signal, all the kids stop in their tracks, look at me, and listen for instructions.

"Thank you for showing me that we need a little more clarity on how to make this helpful and not hurtful. Everyone please stand between the wall and the desks in a big circle facing the center of the room." I wait and they do this. "Now," I say, "check that there is plenty of space—about three or four feet—between the furniture and the wall. If you have to push desks toward the center of the room to create more walk room, please do that now." They do. "Next, if anyone's personal items are in the walkway, please gently shove them under the tables or pick them up and put them on the tables." They do, and I quickly walk around to make sure there is a safe pathway encircling the entire room. "Super! This time, when the music starts, we'll all move in this direction." (I indicate the direction with my hands and body.) "Walk carefully, stay alert, and don't bump into things or people, got it?" They nod. "When the music stops, we stop. After that, we'll stretch."

This time, when I put the music on, there is order. The kids are walking, and soon they are giggling, some are singing along to the song (I'm surprised they know it!), some are hopping as they go, some are skipping, and I'm in the flow with them. As we move along, our bodies naturally pick up the pace, and before long we're all moving quite quickly about the room and it feels wonderful.

The music ends. We all stop where we are and face the center of the room again.

"Henrique," I say, "will you please lead us through some stretches and deep breaths?" He gladly takes up the charge, because he's done this before—they all have—in physical education class. Before long, we're gathering our materials for the day's lesson, and as I look around at all the faces, I can't help but notice how enlivened they are.

Though this wasn't my first time initiating a class to walking around the room, I had forgotten the importance of explaining *how* to move safely around the room before starting the activity. Of course, when I saw the results of my mistake, I could have had the students figure out a solution by asking, "How can we make the room safe for our movement break?" I wish I had done that, because it would've been an opportunity for them to flex their problem-solving muscles *and* gain more ownership over both the space and the activity. Instead, I simply took charge, as you read, and counted myself lucky for having avoided any terrible mishaps caused by my initial oversight.

There are likely to be some bumps in the road to building movement into any classroom, so I'd like to share some of the issues I've both seen and imagined, as well as the solutions I've used as well as some I mentally prepared for but, fortunately, never needed.

When beginning to use movement as a tool for deeper intellectual engagement in your classroom, you may find that students occasionally bump into one another or into furniture (deliberately or accidentally); goof off, ignoring instructions; or experience minor injuries. I've seen a little of this over the years, but these were hiccups easily addressed with conversation about safety and buy-in. I might ask a student, "Would you want to lose the privilege of taking movement breaks because you're not following the safety guidelines?" My approach for any students who make the activity unsafe for themselves or others is to remind them why we have movement breaks, of how they benefit our bodies and minds, and of what an honor it is to be in a classroom—a school—where that kind of activity is encouraged.

Though these instances have been minimal and infrequent in my experience, I still take the potential for them quite seriously. It's important to be prepared for worse, I think, when leading students through movement in the classroom. For that reason, I partnered with my school's physical education teacher, Chris Jacobi. He visited our classroom occasionally and joined us in our movement breaks. He also came by to offer some guidance and remind the kids about all they'd learned in PE about monitoring their own heart rates, being aware of using the space safely, and how to warm up and cool down with stretches. Granted, we weren't exactly running the mile in English language arts (ELA), but these little reminders put my mind at ease and reinforced the guidelines I'd already given my students.

When students did misbehave (I remember one boy named Richard whom I caught trying to trip someone walking in front of him), I sought to correct the behavior rather than remove the child from the activity. The purpose of movement in the classroom is to prepare the brain for complex intellectual tasks. It also releases tension, energizes the body, and elevates the mood, so I believe that "punishing" a student by making him or her sit out the activity is the worst thing to do. The best, in my opinion, is to coach the child toward more appropriate behavior. For example, in Richard's case, I moved to his side and, still walking, said, "Hey, I saw that you just tried to trip Sabrina. That's not going to work."

Richard kept my pace and looked at me. "I'm sorry."

"Well, *sorry* is okay, but what's more important to me is that you do everything in your power to keep yourself and everyone around you safe during our brain breaks. How can you do that?"

As he thought about this, Richard's walking pace slowed a bit. "Well, I can stop trying to trip people."

"That's a great idea. Why is it important to ensure everyone's safety?"

"So they don't get hurt?"

I nodded. "That makes sense to me. Why else?" I felt us slowing down too much, so I picked up the pace and gestured for Richard to keep up.

"Um," he said, "I guess because if people get hurt, we might not be able to do this anymore?"

"Do you think we should be able to keep doing this?"

"I guess. . . ."

"Would you prefer to just sit in your seat all period long and try to do the hard work of ELA without movement breaks?"

He smiled, shook his head, and said, "Not really."

"All right, then. I agree. I think it's important that we all be able to move safely to wake up our brains and make ourselves feel good before getting into the complex work we have to do. So can I trust that you won't try to hurt others again?"

"Yes."

"Great! Thanks, Richard."

We high-fived.

Though it takes more time and attention, this approach works better than a reprimand or consequence, because it positions the students as the thinkers and decision makers, causing them to process the situation more deeply than they would if the adults did all the talking. It also prompts them to consider why movement breaks are beneficial to them. Finally, it demonstrates respect and trust from teachers to students. My mentor, Laura Robb, always reminds me that when we extend trust to our students, they strive to keep that trust intact.

Looking at the previous situation more closely, we can think about how it might've played out differently if I'd simply lectured Richard and assigned a consequence or punishment. When the teacher does all the talking, the student doesn't *have* to really think about the situation. He or she just needs to endure the teacher's speech, nod now and then in an attempt to save face, and move on. If a negative consequence is doled out, the student can build resentment and even anger, but doesn't necessarily think about or strategize how to avoid a repeat performance. He or she might think, as kids sometimes do, that the teacher just doesn't like him or her (a defensive position), which could diminish any incentive to try better next time.

If we consider this further, we might see how treating mishaps with the instinctive scolding plus consequence would cause an undesirable ripple effect. For most adolescents, being reprimanded by a teacher can cause some deeply emotional responses, because kids in the middle grades are sensitive to how others perceive them. When reprimanded or instructed to sit out an activity because of behavioral problems, the student can feel vulnerable or threatened and quickly experience negative stress. This causes the brain to devolve from the higher-order intellectual thinking we'd aimed to nurture with the movement break (and which we want kids to employ in the classroom) to the instinctive, adrenaline-fueled "fight-or-flight" response of the primitive brain (Willis 2010).

When the brain is in this negative, stressed, primitive state, a student will be unable to deeply engage with the intellectual work of the class. Since this is the main goal of our work—and of our movement breaks—we need to be careful about how we handle undesirable behaviors. Giving our "troublemakers" the respect of a conversation positions them in a positive role, empowering them to think and speak for themselves. With no perceived "threat" from us, they are better able to access their higher, evolved brain functions and think up a solution to the problem they created. What's more, students are more likely to follow through with solutions they come up with themselves (or in a partnership with the teacher). This keeps the negative stress at bay and enables the student to then take on the more rigorous intellectual challenges of the academic work after the break.

ACTIVE ENGAGEMENT

Take a brisk walk for five to ten minutes, outdoors if possible, on a treadmill if available. Or spend three to five minutes dancing, jumping, or otherwise moving vigorously.

As soon as your movement ends, help yourself to a glass of water and five minutes with your journal. Write to envision your students in their very first movement session in your classroom (if they haven't already experienced one). What will work? What might be an issue? Who might have the most fun with it? Who might be resistant or skeptical? What can you do to prepare for potential pitfalls?

TALK

It's November and my eighth-grade students and I are in a unit of study on conflict resolution. They're learning strategies for deeply comprehending complex texts. Today's work involves a second reading of an excerpt from a National Geographic (Lancaster 2010) article on nomads in India (we're branching out from texts that are more locally relevant to start considering global issues). The plan for today is to get the students talking in partnerships about what they learn as they apply the strategies of breaking down long sentences and tracking pronoun antecedents to aid comprehension.

As my students work through the text, I circulate to listen in to some partnership conversations. I pause at one table when I hear, "No, it's the British administrators, look!" and I see two girls, Melanie and Rachael, looking intently at a paragraph in the article. I know they are discussing the pronoun antecedent, and I stay to hear the verdict.

"I'm telling you, Rachael, it is not the British administrators—here, let me read it out loud: 'British administrators disparaged them as vagrants and criminals,' so it's saying the administrators disparaged someone else, not themselves. Why would they call themselves criminals?"

Rachael reads more closely, silently.

"You see?" Melanie asks.

Rachael nods, but she's still reading. "Oh, I get it. Them *means the 'wanderers,' but you have to go back to the first sentence in the paragraph to see that. So that means that sometimes the antecedent isn't even in the same sentence!"*

The girls face each other, Rachael looking aghast with her mouth hanging open and Melanie nodding and smiling like she knew it all along. (See Figure 5.4.)

FIGURE 5.4

Giving our students many opportunities to discuss course content allows them to learn how to collaborate honestly and fearlessly.

"Looks like you two just made a discovery," I say. "Nicely done. Would you share that with the others at your table?"

The girls quickly get the others' attention to explain their finding, and I move on to another table where two boys are laughing. I linger to listen in.

"I can't believe they have bear trainers," Jackson says. "Why would they need that? What, do they train the bears to get them fish or something?"

Peter, still laughing, says, "No, they probably train them to do tricks like in a circus."

Jackson notices my presence and says, "Okay, whatever. Let's keep reading."

"Wait, wait," Peter says. "Let's just read this sentence again, because I didn't really get what it was saying. I got stuck on the bear trainers."

Feeling pleased that Peter is monitoring for meaning and conscientious enough to reread when his understanding falters, I keep observing the boys.

Jackson reads aloud: "'The rapidly modernizing India of call centers and brand-obsessed youth has scant use for tinkers or bear trainers, and pastoralists are in a losing battle with industry and urban sprawl.'"

Both boys stare at the page in silence for a few moments.

Jackson begins to read the next sentence, but I ask him to hold off on that. "So what did that sentence mean?"

"Well," Peter ventures, "I guess it's saying that, like . . ."

"Like things are changing in India," Jackson says.

"How are they changing?" I ask.

They both look back at the paper.

"It says, 'The rapidly modernizing India of call centers and brand-obsessed youth,' so it's becoming more modern there, I guess?" Peter says.

"Okay," I say, "and what else does it say?"

Our conversation continues as the boys read the sentence more closely and consider its meaning. By the end, they both understand what the author is saying better than when they nearly moved on in the text before I'd stopped them.

"Did you notice how slowly we went through that one sentence?"

Both boys nod.

"And did you see how it paid off?"

"Yeah, I didn't really know what it meant before," Jackson says.

"And you might've simply read onward, but your confusion would only have grown, because meaning is built sentence by sentence." The boys nod, so I continue. "What did you learn, then, from what we just did?"

Jackson looks at Peter. Peter says, "Just, like . . . slowing down and actually thinking and talking about what's written helps us to actually understand it and that, like . . . it's worth it to take the time to do that because then you know what you're supposed to know by the time you read the whole thing."

I nod and look at Jackson.

"Yeah, and it wasn't really that hard, it's just, it just takes a little time, but it feels good to figure it out," he says.

"Nice work, guys. Keep going," I say, and move along to the next table.

By November, my students are usually accustomed to the collaborative aspect of my class. In September, though, if the kids have not been in a workshop-style classroom previously, they struggle to engage in productive talk with peers. I've found that the best remedy for their hesitation and discomfort is to get them talking often and to coach into their talks frequently. They don't need coaching only in the basic elements of effective conversations; they also need to build trust with one another. Speaking can be a challenge for middle schoolers, because it exposes so much. They can feel vulnerable and insecure. It's only through continued practice that they let down their guard and trust the exploratory nature of much of our work. When this happens, the kids can really build ideas together, but before it happens, they are too cautious to reveal doubt, questions, or confusion about texts they read.

In the previous scenario, Rachael did not hesitate to share her interpretation of the text with Melanie, though she might have if she'd been concerned with being "wrong." Instead, both girls were focused on making an accurate reading of the text and understood that doing so would involve some mistakes along the way. They'd been through enough such processes by then to be comfortable with revealing their uncertainty to their peers. At some point, each person can be wrong and each can be right. What's more important is putting in the effort to learn. If Rachael had held back, the girls might've missed the opportunity to make a discovery about language usage.

Sometimes I wish my students would come to me in September already knowing this and trusting in the process of collaboration—trusting their peers and teachers enough to openly make mistakes and learn from them. But they don't. It takes time. For some, it takes a lot of time. The students working on the nomad article were not new to the workshop method of teaching and learning. They'd had at least three years of workshop-style classrooms in both ELA and social studies. Accountable, productive talk was a big part of their middle school experience. Some of these students even came from elementary schools that used the workshop method (which highly values peer-to-peer discussion and collaboration). All of this is to say that, for them, doing this work was fairly easy. My sixth-grade classes, on the other hand, might not progress quite so quickly. It might be January or February before they have the confidence to reveal their uncertainties to peers in discussions, but I still make sure they have a lot of opportunities to talk each day, because I know it's the only way they'll get there.

I can remember feeling defeated one year in late October, when I created a poetry lesson with three stations. One of the stations was to be a discussion table: the students would discuss the poem they'd read or discuss their thoughts and predictions before reading the poem, depending on when their group reached the station. (I'd done a mini-lesson to build background knowledge and vocabulary for the poem, "Cartoon Physics Part I," by Nick Flynn [Collins 2003]). The poem, describing what ten-year-olds should and shouldn't know, fit perfectly into our narrative unit, which was wrapping up, because through our reading of short stories and writing personal narratives, the kids had been examining issues of identity, fitting in, and the tricky-to-navigate conflict between what kids think they're ready for and what adults think kids are ready for. This lesson, then, would be a chance for the kids to take a break from narrative reading without deviating far from the topics they'd engaged with for nearly a month.

I'd had high hopes for the discussion station, because my students had been doing such a great job with their partner talks that I'd assumed that their success would transfer. When they sat at the discussion station, however, there was more silence than anything else. Some students looked uncomfortably away from the table, and others took to writing in their notebooks. A few attempted to get the conversation started, but their words were swallowed by the quiet. (See Figure 5.5.)

FIGURE 5.5

These students have tools and roles to help their discussion move past "safe" topic-skimming commentary and into the rich territory of analysis and debate. While they are all expected to contribute their interpretations and perspectives of a shared text, they also have accountability and productivity roles: a facilitator, a note-taker, a researcher, and a "respectful language" monitor.

What I'd failed to recognize was that, although the kids had made progress in their partner talks, they were not sitting with their partners at the discussion station. I'd split up the partnerships when I had the students count off to make new groups for the activity. It dawned on me how wise it would've been to make groups of *partnerships* paired together into teams of four or six. That way, there would have been a lot more talk happening at my discussion station, because there would've been a higher level of comfort and familiarity.

My mishap aside, it was painfully clear that my students were not ready in late October to lead deep, thoughtful discussions with their classmates. In subsequent activities, I was more careful to build on the progress they'd already made, but I occasionally mixed things up as I'd done in that poetry stations lesson, just to assess the kids' growth. I found that it could take the entire fall and winter to get students really comfortable with holding collegial discussions with their classmates. And I learned to embrace the process, have patience, and persevere. The payoff is that my students leave my class at the end of the year with more confidence to speak their minds than they had when they arrived in September. They also have more presence to listen to others, and more intellectual stamina to consider someone's statement and add to it, question it, or ask the speaker to elaborate. They are better conversationalists and thinkers. They are more interested in the people and things around them, because they are less intent on blending in.

Each year, when I meet my new students (especially sixth graders, who are new to our school) and ask them to turn and talk to one another, I am reminded of how worthwhile this work is. At the start, they barely make eye contact. They eke out just a word or two, then look at the floor in silence. They may not realize it yet, but they have much to share and to learn.

ACTIVE ENGAGEMENT

Do you have a jump rope? Go ahead and dig it out of that old dusty box in the garage or basement and give it a go. If you can't find a jump rope, pretend you're holding one while you jump with both feet for about three minutes. To add a little brain-building challenge, jump so that your feet land to the right of your center, then to the left. Next, try touching down in front of center, then behind. Stretch and breathe deeply.

Take a few moments to sit down with your lesson plans for the next time you'll be with your students. What will they be working on? What will you be talking about? Whatever the content or task, if you haven't already made peer talk a regular part of your students' classroom experience, go ahead and pencil in a couple of talk breaks for them to process what they've been hearing, seeing, or reading about.

If you already make talk a natural part of your lessons, then take a few moments to reflect in your journal about how it's been going so far and strategize some ways to challenge your students to go deeper in their talks.

MASTER CLASS (BEING INNOVATIVE, RESPONSIVE, AND WILLING TO TRY SOMETHING NEW)

It was the end of our session and the seventh-grade kids were packing their belongings, getting ready to move on to their next class. Kaya came to me and said, "Ms. H., guess what I tried last night."

I smiled and said, "Um, pizza with ice cream on top?"

She laughed. "No. I was doing my homework, and I had a lot, because we have a big social studies project due this week, and anyway, I noticed that I was getting tired, and, like, I couldn't really concentrate anymore, so I decided to get up and take a *brain break*!" So far, I liked where this was going. Kaya continued, "And you know how usually we, like in class, we just walk around or jog in place or whatever?" I nodded. "Well, yeah, I don't know how this idea came to me, but I thought that if I just ran up and down the stairs a couple of times, that would be really good, so I did it and it was incredible, because I actually felt my brain, like, wake up."

"Wow," I said, "I'm so glad you tried this at home and found something that works for you, Kaya, because that means you are tuning in to your own needs and being creative about meeting them. Good for you!" We high-fived.

"Yeah, but I was thinking that, like, since that was so good for me, maybe we can all try it when we take a brain break together."

I thought about it for a moment. "You mean get out of the room and use the stairs?"

She nodded, looking hopeful.

"I will definitely think about it and let you know. One thing I can tell you for sure right now is that it makes me really happy that you are thinking about new ways to get these benefits, not only for yourself, but for the rest of us, too. Thanks for that, Kaya."

She smiled and appeared to grow an extra half inch as she stood before me, then said, "You're welcome."

Kaya's idea stayed with me throughout that afternoon and evening. The next morning, I thought about what it would take to get the kids out of the classroom and into the stairwell during class. Would it offer any additional benefits to their attention and learning readiness? Would it be distracting to other classes in session at that time? Would I be able to monitor for safety?

I thought Kaya's experience was worth testing for everyone. In fact, it made perfect sense to me, since I used the stairs all the time for my own brain breaks during prep periods. She'd said that the result of the stairs exercise was more profound for her than our classroom brain breaks had been to date. Maybe there was something to that. If so, I wanted to know, and I wanted my other students to put it to the test.

Thinking further, I realized my students were already prepared for making the stairwell excursion work: they were expert fire-drill practitioners (moving quickly, silently, and safely); they'd gotten very good at "Spider-man landings" (landing softly on the balls of their feet, rather than on their heels, so they didn't stomp loudly or cause their bodies undue stress); and they'd demonstrated absolute respect for one another's safety in our classroom movement breaks. And just like that, it was a "Go!"

That same day (one day after my talk with Kaya), I announced to our class that we were going to take our brain break in the hallway and that we were going to treat it like a fire drill—moving swiftly, silently, and safely. I cautioned that if we were noisy in the hall or stairwell, we'd immediately return to the room so we wouldn't disturb other classes. The kids welcomed the change, reminding me of the importance of novelty, and appeared willing to accept the conditions I'd laid out.

The hallway was clear and quiet when we stepped into it, and I led my students into the stairwell and up the first flight. I stood at the top and faced my class, waiting for the last students to enter the stairwell. I held my finger to my lips, signaling for silence, and when all eyes were on me, I said, "We'll travel in twos, sticking to the right side of the steps and leaving space for anyone who might be going downstairs. Also: Spider-man landings and keep yourself and everyone around you safe." The kids nodded, and I turned and climbed the steps two at a time for two flights and led the kids into the hallway to walk the length of the school building to the opposite stairwell. Looking behind me, I saw smiling faces, heard some light giggling, and saw a couple of people chatting as they walked, but they were very quiet, so I faced forward again. Into the next stairwell we went, and I swiftly descended the stairs with my students on my tail. The sound they made was more like a breeze than a herd of humans in a stairwell, and I was so proud of them. Back in our own hallway, we walked a little more slowly to calm our breathing and entered our classroom, where we continued to walk until we'd circled the room twice.

I signaled to stop moving and asked my students to remain standing. "Elena, would you please lead us through some stretches?"

Elena did so, and when we finished, I thanked my students for conducting themselves so nicely in our hallways and stairwells.

Then I looked more closely at their faces, which were flushed. Some even glistened with perspiration, indicating that the exercise was indeed more rigorous than our dance and jog breaks even though it hadn't taken us any longer to complete than our classroom jaunts. I felt my own heart pumping harder, too. I asked my class what they thought about our excursion, and they agreed it was invigorating and more rigorous than our usual movement breaks.

Their efforts paid off in class that day, too. We were in a unit of study on Shakespeare's *Romeo and Juliet*, and the students were having a roundtable discussion to explore the question of whether humans are governed by fate or free will. This being April, my students had attempted roundtable discussions before, but those earlier attempts were really more like roundtable shares: anyone who was willing would speak their idea, but I couldn't get the kids to build on what had already been said. It felt as if I'd been coaching into extended discussions endlessly with little lasting improvement, but the pieces really came together on this memorable day. I did my best to stay out of the discussion in the post-staircase brainbreak fate-or-free-will talk, except when needed. My main role was to observe and take notes. On this day, I was practically crossing my fingers in hopes of hearing some of the phrases we'd practiced to help students connect ideas, build on what had already been said, and debate where appropriate. I was listening for phrases such as *I agree with . . . , I see it differently . . . , Will you say more about that? What I'm hearing you say is . . .* , and *That is [the same as or different from] what I got from that part.*

The most remarkable difference in the post-stairwell discussion was how the students connected their statements to what others before them had said, but another difference was the depth with which they explored the concept.

Here's what I transcribed:

TARA: *That question . . . I mean, life is what you make of it and that is all based on your choices, but I mean, I guess there could be fate, too.*

JOHNNY: *It's a conundrum, I think, to agree with what Tara said, because you really can't answer that question. Fate and free will both exist, but you never really know which one is, like, ruling you, you know?*

EVON: *Yeah, I agree with Johnny. You can't really answer that question, but I do think you can spend a lot of time thinking about . . . you know, like trying to understand if any choice you make was really your own choice or if there is a higher power, you know, like if God or whatever is controlling you, or if fate is controlling you, kind of guiding you toward that choice and making you think you made it by yourself or with your free will. . . .*

EMILY: *I think you're right, Evon. I can just imagine myself going crazy trying to figure out where my choices really come from. It might be easier to just not think about it.*

JULIE: *But maybe it isn't one or the other. Maybe we are governed by free will sometimes and by fate other times. Maybe they sort of work together—*

BRENDAN: *Yeah, but Julie, if fate exists at all, then that is the ultimate governing factor, because fate is your ultimate purpose. . . .*

JULIE: *Yeah, fate is the ultimate, but there could still be times when we have free will, because, okay, for example, I can choose what I want to eat for lunch today and that might not really have anything to do with my fate, so fate stays out of that choice. Do you see what I mean?*

BRENDAN: *Well, yes, but if fate can override free will, then does that free will choice really "govern" us or is it just like something we can enjoy once in a while?*

PATTY: *I actually don't think it matters. If fate is the ultimate governing force in our lives, then free will—even if we have it for some things—it doesn't really matter.*

SETH: *I disagree, Patty, because those little free-will choices—and really, they might not all be little choices like what to eat for lunch or whatever, they could be big choices, too, like what job to get and what house to buy and whatnot—but if we do have both, like someone said, then I would think that those free-will choices are the ones that kind of make our daily experience feel like our own. I would think that being able to make our own choices sometimes would help make us have confidence and stuff, you know?*

DANA: *I don't believe in fate at all. I think it's all a hoax. People use "fate" as an excuse for bad behavior or for stupid choices.*

ELLA: *Seriously? Wow, that's harsh, but I hear you. Maybe there is no such thing as fate, but then again, maybe there is no such thing as free will and we're all just fooling ourselves about choices.*

JOHNNY: *What do you mean?*

ELLA: *I mean, look at all the things we have to choose in our lives—how you want to dress, who's your boyfriend, what high school you go to, what career you want—I'm sayin' that maybe we're just fooling ourselves into thinking that we have to make all these choices when really we're gonna be where we're gonna be with who we're gonna be with no matter what we think.*

RITA: *That's a scary thought.*

Did you catch all those practiced talk moves *and then some*? Needless to say, I was beyond pleased with this discussion. And it didn't end there. The conversation continued for twenty-five minutes that day and never slowed. I had to cut the kids off to wrap up the class session. They were still discussing the topic when they filed out of the room, and I was thrilled! What a treat it was to witness their transformation as conversationalists. Though I recognize that many factors were at play, including the fact that this was not the kids' first discussion and that the topic was a meaty one for them, I swore to save the stairwell exercise for days when I had tough tasks planned for these kids, because it seemed to be a kind of magic bullet that ignited a new kind of fire in them. A fire I wanted to see more of!

Another thing I learned from this experience was that I could be more strategic about using movement in different ways at different times for different purposes. I started to look at my students a bit more discerningly and worked harder to be a "close reader" not just of the individuals, but also of the collective.

From that day forth, I learned how to tune in to the energy level in the room and respond appropriately. I didn't go on automatic pilot anymore, starting the class period with movement without checking whether the kids needed it. I also became more strategic and creative with movement breaks, placing them right when and where they were needed rather than just sticking them into the natural transitions of our lessons and class periods. I became more careful about avoiding the same kind of movement more than two days in a row and drew from the kids' experiences (like Kaya's) to add new movement methods to our repertoire every couple of weeks or so.

Over time, I lost my fear of incorporating bold movement into our class sessions. Where once I'd have worried if other adults saw us dancing around the classroom, I later invited them in when they'd peer through our window, curious about our activity. When educators from around the nation came into our class to observe our work, I didn't shy away from doing a brain-break movement session if the kids genuinely needed one that period. I've been able to release control over when and how to do our brain breaks, too, because my students have become adept at monitoring their own needs. They request brain breaks from time to time (when we haven't already done one that day) and even tell me, upon entering the room, "We just came from gym, so we don't need a brain break right now," or "We haven't moved very much today, so can we start with a dance break?"

In the years since I first started using movement to deepen learning experiences in my classroom, I have learned to be responsive to my students' needs in this arena just as I've learned to be responsive to their academic needs. I discovered that when I was willing to try something new, my students usually benefited from it. There were things we tried that didn't work as well, too, like going outside for our brain breaks. I'd figured that the added benefit of "fresh air" (though we were not exactly on the cleanest block in New York City) and some sunshine—not to mention the novelty—would outweigh the hassle of going out, but it didn't. We tried once, but being on the sidewalk felt too unruly. It also took too much time, so I never did that one again. I would in a different setting, though. For example, our school was once housed in a building with a rooftop play space that was safe. I would take my students out there for writing time, but back then I didn't know what I've since learned about movement and the brain. If we had had rooftop access at our newer building, I would definitely have used it for brain breaks.

The following sections offer some ideas for teachers who are ready to be more creative and responsive with movement in the classroom.

SPONTANEOUS MOVEMENT

When you and your students have mastered systematic movement, when it becomes commonplace in your classroom and kids are no longer distracted by the novelty of movement itself, then you can begin to use it as a response to individual and collective energy or engagement levels when needed. For example, you may have a particularly long task for students to complete one day and discover half or three-quarters of the way through that lethargy is setting in. You see students' eyes glazing over, you see heads leaning on hands or desks, you notice one or two kids struggling to stay awake. This is an opportune time to get the kids up. (I'll address test situations in the next section. Right now we are considering lower-stakes tasks that require stamina and longevity.)

If the students must remain silent, such as in a classroom assessment task, you can create a visual signal for them to all stand and stretch (see Figure 5.6). The students could take three deep breaths before returning to the task. You can also invite those who need it most (such as the ones on the verge of napping) to continue their work while standing at the windowsill, where the natural light will enhance the effect of standing and increase their wakefulness.

FIGURE 5.6
When students must do long, silent, seated work, taking stand-and-stretch breaks is a great way to oxygenate the body and brain.

When your students don't have to remain silent, you can tell them to stand up, turn to someone near them, and talk while stretching, or you can simply have them count aloud in unison, following your lead, as they stretch their arms, torsos, and legs. This will definitely help wake them up and oxygenate their brains before returning to the task. Again, allowing some to stand if they need to while working is in everyone's best interest.

This kind of responsiveness to your students will pay off enormously, particularly in extended block periods and afternoon sessions.

It is worth mentioning again that any student who breaks the rules or endangers a classmate during a brain break in my room has to remain in motion *next to me*, rather than dance freely around the room, for the duration of the break. This point is key, because instinctively, we tend to want to "punish" inappropriate behavior. That instinct, though, is a disservice to the whole community, because to take away one of a precious few opportunities to move during the school day only helps build frustration and negativity, which then has no place to go but stews and erupts in another way later on, potentially hurting the student and others.

By the way, this "misbehavior" happened only once or twice in all of my years running a dancing classroom (or, as my students called it, PELA, for physical education language arts). I believe that kids got so much good out of the exercise, they forgot all about their usual need to stir things up in negative ways. Instead, they chose to have fun with the rest of us and to do it safely.

In our class, when the music's on, every student is required to dance their way around the room—teachers do it, too. Many teachers believe their rooms are too crammed with desks and chairs for students to safely dance around in them, and sometimes that is true. In such cases, the students can dance (or jog or hop) in place at their desks. However, I find more often that there is plenty of room but we teachers may need to observe our rooms more creatively. Sometimes the furniture can be rearranged or there is an abundance of wasted space that can be used. It just takes an open mind and a bit of creativity to make a movement-friendly space (see Chapter 2 for more on this). And if you're ever stuck, turn to the experts: the students. If you tell them you want to create a safe environment for them to move in, they will have your room transformed within five minutes. Voila!

You might be tempted to think that brain breaks like these—especially with music!—would be so disruptive that getting kids back to task afterward would be impossible. Well, no. Actually, the opposite is true. My students have found the music breaks to be so much fun, and such an effective tension reliever and energizer, that they have been *more* motivated to finish their work and better able to focus afterward. It is quite possible that they are so appreciative of the chance to let loose in the middle of the school day, even for just a few minutes, that they give more attention to your teaching afterward and try harder to participate in the work. It's almost as though their effort is the return on your investment in fun. I'll point out, too, that once we were using movement regularly in my ELA class, students rarely asked to leave for bathroom breaks (which are, more often than not, just a desperate plea for a mental break and the chance to stretch the legs).

This is consistent with Dr. John Ratey's research on active students: After exercise, "They are prepared to learn, . . . their senses are heightened; their focus and mood are improved; they're less fidgety and tense; and they feel more motivated and invigorated" (2008, 35).

I'd like to inject a word about making this work: if you, the leader of the classroom activities, stand watching the kids eagle-eyed with your arms folded across your chest, or in any other way convey a negative or authoritative message, the kids will not engage themselves effectively in the exercise. As with so many things in teaching, when we model the behavior we expect from the kids, they are more willing to participate. Frankly, whatever our behavior, it serves as a model in the kids' eyes, so if we stand still and stiff but tell them to move and have fun, we're sending a mixed signal and kids get confused and uncomfortable. Besides, the effects of exercise are universal: it improves our mood and mental sharpness just as it does our students'.

MOVEMENT AND HIGH-STAKES TESTS

As I mentioned, testing situations require a different strategy for increasing mental alertness. When you observe lethargy taking over during a classroom test, you can decide if you want to lead the whole class through a silent stretch session in which all eyes are on you and students understand their responsibility to avoid looking at others' papers or if you want to allow kids to get up as needed, provided they don't look at others' work or distract peers. If the lethargy descends during a high-stakes test, however, options are more limited (see Figure 5.7). Students should have a number of personally effective strategies upon which to draw so they can combat the mental fatigue and reenergize themselves without violating testing conditions and rules or distracting others. This requires planning and a lot of practice. Providing the time to try out numerous methods was always one major focus of my test-prep unit. Kids learned to build stamina for longer-duration tasks and practiced revitalizing strategies until they knew which ones worked best for them and could use them independently. At the end of this section, I've listed the strategies that most of my students found useful.

With all the anxiety around testing, educators can be nervous about employing nonstandard methods of attention management when tests roll around. We don't want to try new things at this juncture in the year; we need to be confident in our methods and ensure that our students have some sense of normalcy in the testing season. By that same token, this is also not the time to stop using effective methods that have served the students well throughout the year.

In the weeks before standardized tests roll around, many of us spend some time preparing students for the unique demands of the test. Some of us do no test prep at all. Yet others of us use that time to quickly cover a few more topics in our subject area, hoping the exposure will somehow pay off if the test presents a question or two pertaining to those topics. I prefer to spend that time building stamina and test-taking skills, such as reading a variety of short, complex texts in a timed period; deciphering exactly what kind of information questions are asking for (summary, inference, text evidence, definitions, comparisons, etc.); answering a question before looking at the answer choices (which are designed to confuse test takers); and composing effective short and extended responses to a variety of text-based prompts. I also spend a good deal of time helping students adapt our movement practices for the testing situation.

FIGURE 5.7
High-stakes exams can tire out the body and brain. Keeping the body oxygenated and the brain activated requires some savvy strategy.

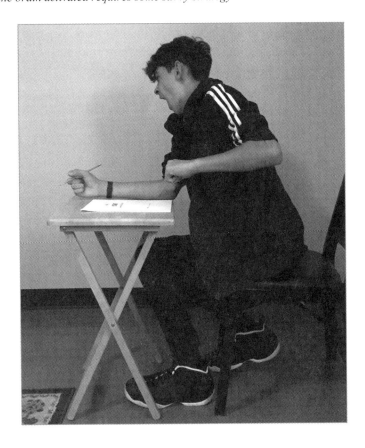

This last bit has enormous payoff. Many of our students who identify as "knowledgeable and skilled, but not good test takers" experience stress during tests. Whatever the source of the stress, if they have no management skills for it, their test performance suffers. I believe that many of those students perform better if they can independently manage their energy and attention during the test. Students who don't stand out as particularly troubled during testing situations benefit, too. Being equipped with the strategies to maximize their focus, manage their energy, and meet their own unique needs independently while attending to the intellectual demands of the test are valuable to anyone who sits for a high-stakes test.

Again, I employ a gradual release model with this self-management (movement and mindfulness) work, so that by the end of our test-prep mini-unit of study, when students experience a mock-test session, they can independently apply the strategies that work best for them.

When preparing our students for standardized tests, then, we can think about our work differently from how we might've in the past. We can think about the various tasks and pressures, both intellectual and physical, that come along with those tests. For example, during a high-stakes test session, our students will face long stretches of sitting still, remaining silent, concentrating deeply, and demonstrating complete independence—not to mention the restrictive setting (and that heavy weight in the air), which can be distracting to some. They'll face the stress of wondering if they're working fast enough, if they should slow down, if others are ahead or behind them in the test, if they'll finish on time, if they'll have a chance to check their work. They'll also face baffling questions and confusing answer choices, complicated texts, deceptively simple problems (and deceptively complex ones), and often unclear expectations, not to mention the ticking clock. When we consider all of this, we can appreciate the value of using class time to prepare our students to manage all of it independently.

A colleague of mine is, at this moment, sitting down for (yet another) standardized test on physics to keep her science teaching certification current. When we talked about the test, she explained how she'd prepare for this one: "I'm going to make sure I get a full night's sleep the night before. I'm going to do a complete yoga session in the morning and get a full breakfast. I'm going to bring water and have snacks on hand for before and after the test, and I'm going to get up and go to the bathroom when my brain needs a break." She's already an expert in her content area, so that "prep" work is done. She is a successful test taker, not just because she knows her content, but because she goes in prepared for the situation. She knows what to expect. She knows what her body and mind will need to stay focused and meet the intellectual and physical demands of the task. She knows this because she's been through many such situations before and has learned from them. Our students, on the other hand—especially middle schoolers who are still fairly new to standardized testing—may not have learned yet how to keep themselves energized and mentally alert for long testing sessions. Helping them do so is, I believe, an important part of our job.

We know how to prepare our students for the content and academic skills they'll encounter and demonstrate on the test. Preparing them for the physical demands takes a little more finesse.

If movement has become commonplace in the classroom environment, students are familiar with the concept behind the practice: moving the body helps the brain think more clearly. Now we just need to teach them how and when they can use that knowledge to improve their test-taking experience. We can use the weeks before the big test to let kids practice a number of testing-environment-friendly strategies that they can employ as needed, both independently and with grace, since they must avoid being a distraction to other test takers.

Giving the students a number of different options is key, because not all methods will work for everyone. What's most important is that we convey to students the necessity of discovering what works for them individually, so they can all be ready to master their own experience.

One way to think about using movement to benefit testing is to consider *when* and *where* as opposed to *what* methods to use. We already know that rigorous cardiovascular movement wakes up the brain, so we need to strategize when and where to do it on testing days. We also know that the greatest benefits are achieved when movement happens before cognitive challenge. If movement is going to happen before the test is administered, then students should be prepared to do some of this on their own, before arriving at school, since state tests usually begin at the start of the school day. There are also ways to build in brief movement sessions together, before the test begins. The following strategies will prepare the brain for the intellectual work of standardized testing:

1. **Before School**
    These four strategies can be shared with students, because they directly address the kids.

    a. Incorporate jumping jacks and stretches into the morning routine.

    b. Dance or hop while choosing your outfit.

    c. Walk briskly to the bus stop or to school. If someone drives you to school, consider leaving five minutes early and using that time to walk outside.

    d. Jog in place while waiting for the bus. If someone drives you, jog in place, dance, or do jumping jacks while waiting for him or her to get the car ready.

2. **At School, Before the Test**
    The whole class can do these together, or everyone in the building can be involved. A whole-school pre-test exercise session is highly effective for decreasing pre-test anxiety, preparing the brain for intellectual challenge, and readying the body for the physical demands ahead. At the Clinton School for Writers and Artists, our physical education teacher, Chris Jacobi, directs us through exercises and stretches from the loudspeaker. This allows students to get into their testing rooms first, do their brain-enhancing movement, and settle in for the long session without losing any time in transitions. It also ensures that everyone has the space needed to do the moves, which would be harder to accomplish if we all crowded into the gymnasium. Because

the test session is so long, and because we know that it takes approximately twenty minutes to fully awaken the brain's cognitive function, devoting ten to twenty minutes to this is ideal. Chris leads us through fifteen minutes of heart-pumping moves and then cool-down stretches. Finally, I have my students write for three minutes to warm up their cognitive function and writing muscles as much as to relieve any residual stress about the test. Here are some steps I suggest for pre-test movement in school:

a. Direct students to their testing room with twenty to twenty-five minutes to spare before the official start time of the exams.

b. If the school supports a unified experience, a coach can lead the exercises from a loudspeaker or via videoconferencing tool.

c. If you're on your own for this, you can use the same moves you've been using since September to get kids' blood flowing. Note: If you want to use music for this, finding upbeat tunes without lyrics is a good idea, since lyrics may influence students' thinking. This will be an important time for them to tune in to their own thoughts.

d. Spend approximately fifteen minutes in movement and allow for three minutes or so to stretch.

e. Students may need water and a chance to use the restroom before settling in for the test.

3. **At School, After the Test**
When the test is over, the regular school day begins. Before jumping into the next lesson (or, heaven forbid, quiz—my son has actually had classroom tests and quizzes on the same day he sat for standardized tests;

please don't do this to your students), help your students release the test tensions and prepare for new learning with a movement break. If you can do this outdoors, all the better.

a. When all the exams have been collected, dedicate as much as ten minutes for movement and talk.

b. Consider getting the kids moving for the duration of one upbeat song. (Mark Ronson's "Uptown Funk" is great for this!)

c. After the music, lead students through some simple stretches, and then instruct them to "mingle" (they can remain standing or stroll around the room while talking with partners). Either provide a prompt for the talk (related to upcoming work or in reflection of the exam) or allow students to determine their own topics. I've found that this is an excellent time for kids to talk about what self-management strategies worked for them and what they'll do differently during the next day's test.

4. **After School**
Students might consider taking a long bike ride, walk, or run after school (with parents' approval, of course). This will serve to work out any residual stress from the taxing test while getting the body and brain ready to relax for the evening. I like to share the at-home suggestions with parents at the start of our test-prep unit and then a brief reminder a few days before the test, so they can be partners in this work (or at least aware of why their child is suddenly so intent on dancing before school!).

Vigorous movement before and after the test will be effective, but students will also need ways to manage their energy and focus *during* the test. This is where absolute discretion becomes essential, and this is the stuff our students will need to practice during test-prep weeks. Having moved vigorously before the test, students will find that simple breathing and stretching breaks will provide powerful relief from the kinks that can set in during long, silent, seated sessions, as well as from the mental strain of continually applied concentration. If students haven't moved before sitting for a test, they will benefit from the more vigorous, out-of-room breaks included in the list below.

Here are some tried-and-true strategies—no doubt each of you and your students will come up with others to add to the list:

1. **Simple Breathing Break**
   This is great for students who are beginning to feel stressed or unfocused but are not yet in need of stretching.

   a. Put down pen or pencil, and sit with back straight and feet flat on floor.

   b. Close eyes and inhale deeply through the nose. Hold breath in full lungs for a count of three, and then exhale completely through nose.

   c. Repeat two times. Let breathing return to normal and, when ready, gently open eyes.

   d. Return attention to test.

2. **Closed-Eyes, In-Chair Stretch**
   The closed eyes ensure that a student cannot be accused of looking at others' papers, but this method also helps give the eyes a much-needed rest. Students who wear eyeglasses should remove them before this exercise.

   a. Turn over test paper (only if this is not the local signal that work is finished and the teacher should take the paper away) and put down pencil or pen.

ACTIVATE

b. Close eyes, sit tall, and reach hands high above head; arch back if that feels good. Drop hands to sides.

c. Gently, slowly, twist torso to the right while stretching right arm behind body and left arm across front of body (see Figure 5.8). Slowly twist back to center.

d. Inhale to fill lungs and ribs; exhale completely.

e. Repeat twist on left side (left arm goes behind, right arm across front of body). Return to center.

f. Take another deep inhalation and exhalation.

g. Nod head slowly forward and backward, and then (eyes still closed) turn from side to side. Take a final slow, deep inhalation. Exhale completely.

h. Open eyes and return attention to the test.

3. **Arms, Wrists, Hands, and Fingers Stretch**
This is ideal for cramped muscles in the writing hand, but doing the stretches with both arms is key for balance and redistribution of energy.

a. Put down pencil or pen. Eyes can remain open or students may choose to close them. Note: Open-eyed students should be in the habit of looking above the heads of peers to avoid being accused of cheating. Never let eyesight drop into the range of classmates' papers.

b. Interlock fingers and stretch hands as far in front of you as possible with a straight back (see Figures 5.9 A and B). Without straining the shoulders, elbows, or wrists, hold this position for the duration of one deep inhalation and exhalation. Release arms. You may repeat the stretch with the hands facing the opposite direction. (If palms were out before, this time stretch arms out in front with palms facing inward.)

FIGURE 5.8
Stretching in the chair helps rejuvenate focus, alleviate body stiffness, and reenergize the brain.

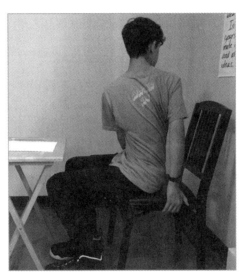

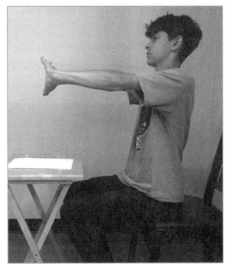

FIGURE 5.9A, 5.9B
Arms, wrists, and fingers stretches

c. Next, reach arms overhead and take one deep breath. While exhaling, lean slightly to the right. Inhale while straightening back to center (arms still raised). Repeat on the left to stretch side, and return to center.

d. With arms still above head, bend one elbow, allowing the hand to drop behind the back. Place the opposite hand on the bent elbow, providing gentle downward pressure. This stretches the triceps. Throughout the stretch, inhale and exhale deeply. Repeat on the other side.

e. Let arms fall to sides. Shake them out if that feels good.

f. Next, cross one arm in front of the chest and provide gentle pressure on the upper arm with the opposite hand, stretching the back and shoulder (see Figure 5.10). Hold for one deep breath. Repeat for the other arm.

FIGURE 5.10
Cross-chest arm stretch

g. With arms hanging at your sides, gently bend each hand backward, to stretch the inner wrist, and then forward to stretch the outer wrist. Repeat the backward-forward motion until wrists feel loose.

h. Finally, squeeze both hands into tight fists, then open as wide as possible, spreading the fingers as far apart as they will go. Repeat this closed-open sequence until fingers and hands feel loose and energized.

i. Shake out arms and hands.

j. Return attention to test.

4. **Leg Stretch**
This is especially helpful for students who get fidgety when sitting for long periods, but is also good for anyone who feels an overall sense of lethargy. This stretch helps alleviate problems when getting up for a bathroom break is not feasible.

a. Students begin by putting down their pen or pencil. Stabilize the torso by holding on to the side edges of the seat or desk and then stretch the legs straight out in front with feet lifted off the floor. Bend knees and return feet to floor. Repeat this move two or three times until legs feel a bit more loose and awake.

b. Next, place feet flat on floor with knees at a ninety-degree angle. Lift toes up, stretching ankles and calves, then release toes to the floor. Repeat this move until the ankles and calves feel awake and loosened. Keep breathing deeply throughout all of these stretches, and remember to keep eyes away from peers' papers.

c. Next, lift heels up, then release down and repeat a few times.

d. Finally, shift to the right of the chair until your right buttock is off the chair, but keep your left one firmly planted. Hold on to the chair with left hand while grabbing right ankle in right hand. Gently pull the right ankle backward until the right knee is pointing down toward the floor and you can feel a stretch in the right thigh and shin (see Figure 5.11). Hold for one to three deep breaths and gently release. Repeat on the left side.

e. Center yourself in the chair again, and take one more deep breath (preferably with eyes closed).

f. Return attention to the test.

5. **Combination**
Students will become adept at assessing their attention, energy levels, and needs. Soon they will be comfortable with these moves and create the exact combination they need to reenergize their bodies and brains and to refocus their attention. Any one stretch described above may be enough to get a student refocused, just as any combination may work.

6. **What strategies can you or your students add to the list?**

7. **Bathroom Break**
This is the tried-and-true student default. Now that students have other methods of stretching, they won't depend as heavily on the bathroom break, but we can teach them to add this to their repertoire with some pumped-up tweaks.

a. Make this break really count by walking as quickly as possible once you've left the testing room, and by using the stairs if allowed.

b. In the bathroom, students can do a few jumping jacks and stretches.

c. When washing hands, let some cool water flow over the insides of your wrists. This helps wake up a drowsy brain.

d. Be sure to get a drink of water before returning to the test room.

Having made the connection between how our physical movement supports our brain function, I have no doubt you'll discover opportunities for incorporating movement into your class sessions, as will your students. Being a master at this means being open to the possibilities and willing to try them out.

FIGURE 5.11
Seated leg stretch. Students need to practice this carefully and avoid letting the chair tip over.

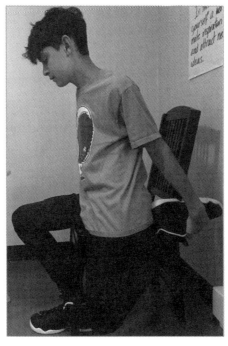

ACTIVE ENGAGEMENT

Take up to twenty minutes to engage in your favorite movement activity (for example, walking, dancing, jogging) and treat yourself to stretches and a drink of water afterward.

Allow yourself five minutes or so to write a reflection in your journal, using some or all of the following prompts and guiding questions:

- Before reading this book, I thought that classroom activities should be . . . Now I think . . .

- Since starting this book, I have increased my students' talk and movement opportunities by . . .

- As a class, we are now regularly using the following movement and talk strategies . . .

- Since adding more movement and talk to our class sessions, I've noticed that my students and I . . .

- What are my students saying about how the movement and extra talk time affects them, their learning, their productivity, their focus, and their grades?

- How can I invite my students to take more ownership of managing their energy and focus?

- How can I raise the level of effectiveness of our classroom movement and talk, now that we've become comfortable with using these methods?

- What questions do I still have? How can I find answers to them?

CLOSING

FROM WHAT TO HOW WE TEACH

Teaching in the middle grades is a unique privilege with particular responsibilities. Our students vacillate between elementary and mature behaviors and attitudes throughout the day, and we get to be there to support them through it all. One minute they are practically begging for more autonomy, and the next they are wondering why we aren't guiding their every step. One minute they're having a sophisticated discussion about classic literature or social issues, and the next they can't control their laughter over something trivial and silly. One day they are lamenting the loss of a childhood toy, and the next they're elated over attention from a crush.

On the cusp of teenhood, these kids are grappling with blurry social lines that just a year or two earlier were clear. The rules of the game are fluid and uncertain in early adolescence. The kids themselves are finding their voices and yet wary of expressing them. It's a tenuous stage of identity building in which kids are just coming out from the shadow of their parents' version of who they are to claim their own stakes on their "me"-ness. Our teaching is necessarily about much more than our content expertise. It has to be about the kids themselves.

In the early days of my teaching, I thought of myself as an English language arts teacher, first and foremost. In that mind-set, the course content took priority in my classroom. Everything the students and I did was in service to learning the content. Over the years, though, I came to see that my teaching is about the kids first and that my course content is taught in service of the kids' personal development and well-being. To me, this means that a big part of my job is helping my students navigate this middle terrain with increasing confidence and authenticity, building skills that will serve their continued growth beyond my tenure in their lives. It means helping them understand how their bodies and brains work, and it means helping them find their own voices and honor their own experiences and perspectives. It means helping them learn to listen well and honor others' experiences and perspectives. And it means finding course materials that will serve them well, and teaching them how to find relevant materials on their own.

Which brings me to another privilege of my work as a literacy specialist: I *can* tailor my course content to reflect the particular characteristics, interests, and needs of my students, both individually and collectively. For example, one year an overwhelming majority of my students were high-achieving girls with strong literacy skills and backgrounds. That year, my students designed independent studies, researched topics and issues of interest, and demonstrated their learning in presentations that included videos, novellas, informational books, and graphic fiction (like comics). Another year, a large portion of my students were struggling to average in literacy skills, so we spent more time on building interest and personal motivation to read and write, finding books, articles, music, interviews, and films that helped the kids make connections between literacy and life achievement. They presented their learning in speeches, essays, blog posts, original songs, poetry collections, and short fiction.

In some ways, I've felt (now and then) that I've enjoyed an unfair advantage over my colleagues who teach math, science, and social studies, because they have less choice about *what* they teach. On the other hand, I've also envied their content limitations, because they don't have drastic changes in course material from year to year. Curating new materials, designing original units of study and lesson plans, and creating new rubrics to go along with all of that every year is no small task for me. My summers, weekends, evenings, and holiday recesses are rarely work-free. I suppose I *could* teach the same content from year to year, but that would feel like cheating—cheating my students out of a tailor-made curriculum that reflects them in some way, and cheating myself of the inspiration, passion, and pride that comes with innovation and continual growth. Besides, once I've used a certain text, lesson sequence, or rubric, I always find ways to improve it for future use.

Over the years, I've learned that what matters more than the content we teach is *how* we teach. The ways in which we connect with our students, treat them, and share our time and space with them eclipses any information they will add to their knowledge base in the year or years they spend with us. Their school day can nurture and respect their humanness, their well-being, and their growing sense of self-efficacy. They can walk away from their time with us knowing a little more about themselves and how to navigate the world they live in.

Regardless of the content, my students all work on the skills associated with the key concepts I've developed throughout this book: understanding the body-brain connection; harnessing the power of effective verbal (and written) communication; and being cognizant of how novelty affects our attention (as well as, of course, recognizing how literature contributes to life experience). With these skills, they can lead themselves toward their personal goals. My goal is for my students to end the year knowing more about themselves, and more about how they can take ownership over their education and life, than they knew when they started.

At the beginning of this book, I wrote about my academically successful students lacking an edge and my not knowing what that edge was or where it would come from. After changing *how* I teach by releasing control, incorporating deliberate brain-stimulating movement, and creating a dynamic and flexible learning space, I no longer have that nagging feeling that I've missed something or that my students aren't getting maximum benefit from their time with me. They are more deeply engaged, they're happy, and they're taking ownership over—and pride in—their learning.

What could be better?

Bibliography

Allen, Janet. 1999. *Words, Words, Words: Teaching Vocabulary in Grades 4–12*. York, ME: Stenhouse.

Baker, Scott K., Deborah C. Simmons, and Edward J. Kameenui. 1995. *Vocabulary Acquisition: Synthesis of the Research*. Eugene, OR: National Center to Improve the Tools of Educators, College of Education, University of Oregon.

Barbieri, Maureen. 1995. *Sounds from the Heart: Learning to Listen to Girls*. Portsmouth, NH: Heinemann.

Bowman, Katy. 2014. *Move Your DNA: Restore Your Health Through Natural Movement*. Carlsborg, WA: Propriometrics Press.

Brown, Jennifer. 2009. *Hate List*. New York: Little, Brown.

Burkins, Jan Miller, and Kim Yaris. 2016. *Who's Doing the Work? How to Say Less So Readers Can Do More*. Portland, ME: Stenhouse.

Calkins, Lucy. 2014. *A Guide to the Common Core Writing Workshop, Middle School Grades*. Portsmouth, NH: Heinemann.

Collins, Billy. 2003. *Poetry 180: A Turning Back to Poetry*. New York: Random House Trade Paperbacks.

Copeland, Matt. 2005. *Socratic Circles: Fostering Critical and Creative Thinking in Middle and High School*. Portland, ME: Stenhouse.

Cunningham, Katie Egan. 2015. *Story: Still the Heart of Literacy Learning*. Portland, ME: Stenhouse.

Dewey, John. 2015. *Experience and Education*. New York: Free Press.

Diamond, Marion Cleeves. 2001. "Response of the Brain to Enrichment." http://lunaproductions.com/wp-content/uploads/2014/05/Response-of-Brain-to-Enrichment.pdf.

Hattie, John. 2012. *Visible Learning for Teachers: Maximizing Impact on Learning*. London: Routledge.

Heal, Jim. March 28, 2014. "How Harkness Works." https://www.youtube.com/watch?v=dKnVteBrdLw.

Jensen, Frances E., and Amy Ellis Nutt. 2015. *The Teenage Brain: A Neuroscientist's Survival Guide to Raising Adolescents and Young Adults*. New York: HarperCollins.

Johnston, Peter H. 2012. *Opening Minds: Using Language to Change Lives*. Portland, ME: Stenhouse.

Lancaster, John. 2010. "India's Nomads." National Geographic. http://ngm.nationalgeographic.com/2010/02/nomads/lancaster-text.

Levine, James A. 2014. *Get Up! Why Your Chair Is Killing You and What You Can Do About It*. New York: Palgrave Macmillan.

Lewis, Katherine Reynolds. 2017. "Everything You Think You Know About Disciplining Kids Is Wrong." Mother Jones, June 29. http://www.motherjones.com/politics/2015/07/schools-behavior-discipline-collaborative-proactive-solutions-ross-greene/.

Marzano, Robert J. 2009. "The Art and Science of Teaching / Six Steps to Better Vocabulary Instruction." http://www.ascd.org/publications/educational-leadership/sept09/vol67/num01/Six-Steps-to-Better-Vocabulary-Instruction.aspx.

Mayher, John Sawyer. 1990. *Uncommon Sense: Theoretical Practice in Language Education*. Portsmouth, NH: Boynton/Cook.

Medina, John. 2011. *Brain Rules: 12 Principles for Surviving and Thriving at Work, Home, and School.* Seattle, WA: Pear Press.

Mercer, Neil. 2012. "Dialogues for Learning." Filmed at The University of Northampton Learning and Teaching Conference 2010, Northampton, United Kingdom. Video, 41:16. https://youtu.be/wtuQsKOr47k.

Phelps, James. 2014. "Memory, Learning, and Emotion: the Hippocampus." PsychEducation. http://psycheducation.org/brain-tours/memory-learning-and-emotion-the-hippocampus/.

Phillips Exeter Academy. "Harkness History." http://webqa.exeter.edu/admissions/109_1220_11688.aspx.

"R.A.D. by Judy Willis M.D., M.Ed." http://www.radteach.com/.

Ratey, John J., and Eric Hagerman. 2008. *Spark: The Revolutionary New Science of Exercise and the Brain*. New York: Little, Brown.

Robb, Laura. 1999. *Easy Mini-Lessons for Building Vocabulary.* New York: Scholastic.

—. 2013. *Unlocking Complex Texts: A Systematic Framework for Building Adolescents' Comprehension*. New York: Scholastic.

Schlorff, Anthony. "Learning Readiness PE." http://learningreadinesspe.com/.

Sitomer, Alan Lawrence. 2008. *Teaching Teens and Reaping Results*: Stories, Strategies, Tools and Tips from a Three-Time Teacher of the Year Award Winner*. New York: Scholastic.

Suzuki, Wendy. 2011. "Exercise and the Brain." Filmed November 2011 at TEDxOrlando, Orlando, FL. Video, 14:02. http://www.wendysuzuki.com/media-video-gallery/2016/1/30/tedxorlando-wendy-suzuki-exercise-and-the-brain.

Tharp, Roland G., and Ronald Gallimore. 1988. *Rousing Minds to Life: Teaching, Learning, and Schooling in Social Context*. Cambridge: Cambridge University Press.

Van Praag, Henriette, Gerd Kempermann, and Fred H. Gage. 2001. "Neural Consequences of Environmental Enrichment." https://www.researchgate.net/publication/12074538_Van_Praag_H_Kermpermann_G_Gage_FH_Neural_consequences_of_environmental_enrichment_Nat_Rev_Neurosci_1_191-198.

Vygotsky, L. S., and Alex Kozulin. 1986. *Thought and Language*. Cambridge, MA: MIT Press.

Willis, Judy. 2010. "What to Do When Your Child Hates School." Psychology Today. https://www.psychologytoday.com/blog/radical-teaching/201007/what-do-when-your-child-hates-school.

—. 2013. "Video Game MODEL for Motivated Learning." Filmed January 2013 at TEDxASB. https://www.youtube.com/watch?v=i8TPRec6OCY.

WNYC. 2013. "Guilty Until Proven Innocent." http://www.wnyc.org/story/guilty-until-proven-innocent/.

Wormeli, Rick. 2001. *Meet Me in the Middle: Becoming an Accomplished Middle-Level Teacher*. Portland, ME: Stenhouse.

Yancey, Antronette. 2012. "What's Good for the Waistline Is Good for the Bottom Line." Filmed October 2012 at TEDxManhattanBeach, Manhattan Beach, CA. Video, 12:40. http://tedxmanhattanbeach.com/past-events/october-2012-conference-journey-to-purpose/presenters/toni-yancey/.

Index

INDEX

frequent alterations and, 76-77
manipulation and, 74
neurological cues and, 84
new seating arrangements and, 76
new units of study and, 81-84
off-limit areas and, 76
setting up early, 72
territorial ownership and, 77
See also room rearrangements
Pop Quiz Catch, movement and, 58
predictability, 44
punishment, 124

R
Ratey, J., 143
Spark, 8, 18-19
receptor stimulation, learning and, 40-41
revitalizing strategies, 144
Robb, L., 30, 54, 69, 113
room arrangements
administration opposition and, 86
changing peer partnerships and, 86
content change and, 86-87
content support and, 87
examples of, 88-90
flexibility and, 91-97
furniture, amount of and, 94
sound and, 85
stationary furniture and, 85
subtle changes and, 84-85
teachers demeanor and, 96
time constraints and, 85-86
See also physical environment
routines, changing, 8-9

S
Scavengers, movement and, 58
Simmons, D.C., 30
simple breathing breaks, 151
Sitomer, A., 51-52
sitting, standing versus, 9
sitting disease, 20
Socrates, 28
Socrates Circles, (Copeland), 36
Spark,(Ratey), 8, 18-19
spontaneity, room arrangements and, 91-97
See also physical environment; room
arrangements
spontaneous flexibility , 91-97
fluid thinking and, 92-93
spontaneous movement, 140-143
stairwell movement, 134-135
standardized test strategies, 146-148
after school, 150
afterwards, 149-150
before school, 148
before the test, 148-149
during test and, 150-157
Stand If You Please, movement and, 59
Standing Room Only, movement and, 58
standing workstation, concept of, 101

student talk, class control and, 106-107
Suzuki, W., 17, 23-25

T
talk, 126-129
collaboration and, 129-130
discussion and, 29, 31
discussion stations and, 130-132
hesitation and, 129
learning and, 25-32
memory and, 25
neurological competence and, 37
talk moves and, 29
teacher learning journal, 5-6
teachers, coaching and, 68-70
territorial ownership, 77-78
test-taking strategies, 143-146, 147-148
test-taking strategies, during test
arms, wrists, hands, finger stretch, 152-155
bathroom break, 156-157
closed-eyes, in-chair stretch, 151-152
combination, 156
leg stretches , 155-156
simple breathing break, 151
Tharp, R.G., 31
timed mingle, 52
transitions, 11
Turn-and-Talk (T&T), movement and, 26, 57, 59

U
Uncommon Sense, (Mayher), 35-36

V
Van Praag, H., 40
verbal engagement, short bursts and, 27-28
vocabulary
domain-specific, 29
instruction, 30
Vygotsky, L., 29

W
walk and talk
illustration of, 49-51
insights from, 51
introducing, 49
variations, 52
Walkie Talkie, movement and, 57
warm-up activity time, 48
Who's Doing the Work? (Burkins & Yaris), 68-69
Willis, J., 42, 77-78, 125
Wordgen.serpmedia.org, 29
workshop method, teaching and, 11
writing, learning and, 25
www.learningreadinesspe.com, 19

Y
Yancey, A., 23

Z
Zone Shift, movement and, 58